The Cultural Theology
Of Bernard E. Meland

FAITH
AND
APPRECIATIVE
AWARENESS

J. J. Mueller, S.J.
Gonzaga University

UNIVERSITY
PRESS OF
AMERICA

Library of Congress Catalog Card Number: 80-5969

To my father and mother—John and Cecelia Mueller

where my learning began

"No man is an island," wrote the poet-churchman, John Donne. Might he not better have said, Every man is an island, but islands are not what they appear to be: isolated bodies of land. For if one presses beneath the surface of the water one will come upon a land base that unites these individual bodies of land with all land.

Bernard E. Meland

TABLE OF CONTENTS

FOREWORD

In this book Dr. Mueller undertakes a probing and sympathetic inquiry into my thought, addressing himself specifically to two themes: Appreciative Awareness and Faith, which he considers basic to understanding my mode of theological inquiry. He further restricts the scope of his work by focusing attention upon three works: *Faith and Culture* (1953), *The Realities of Faith* (1962), and *Fallible Forms and Symbols* (1976). Both procedures are appropriate. In any selective account of this sort, however, one must ignore, or at least diminish the genetic account of the story. And without its orientation, the import of preliminary strands of inquiry and influence, at work more hiddenly, must go unattended.

I.

My concern with appreciative awareness and faith did not emerge whole-cloth in the nineteen-fifties. It had been evoked initially by a shift in perspective, following from fresh impulses or thought that were emerging in theology and philosophy during the nineteen-twenties. By that time the import of relativity was being discussed in areas of thought outside the sciences; while scientists, notably physicists, in their study of wave particles, were countering the mechanistic view of Nature, which had held sway since the time of Newton. A new, mysterious universe was coming into view: creative of all enduring existence, yet not wholly identifiable with its various levels of creatural existence; not even with the human level in all respects. Besides dispelling the mechanistic view of nature, this new vision of science seemed to render modern forms of Humanism and Idealism suspect insofar as their means of reacting against a mechanistic view of Nature during former years had taken the form of idealizing *human* nature. In Personal Idealism, for example, mind, personality, and ideals became themselves the criteria for identifying the nature of God. *Imago-humanitas* had supplanted *Imago-dei*. It was during these years that the phrase, "Recovering The Objective Mood" became dominant and impelling. That theme became dominant in my writing as well, and remained so through subsequent years. In that context, *sense of wonder* as a state of open awareness became an initial rhythm of inquiry, followed by the meaning and role of creaturehood.

The trilogy, beginning with *Faith and Culture* in 1953, marked a new stage in reorienting human inquiry. There it was not so much new disclosures in nature, impelling an objective mood, though that theme persisted with ascending import; rather it was heinous disclosures of evil and horror within the human community which awakened that generation of scholars, scientists, churchmen and clergy, poets and philosophers, along with the daily press and the public at large, to an unprecedented sense of guilt and despair following the falling of bombs, and disclosures of Auschwitz, Buchenwald, and Dachau. Appreciative awareness and Faith seem tepid words to relate to such trauma and despair. Yet it was in that context that *despair of life* was coupled with the earlier theme *in praise of life*. Both were seen as being expressive of creaturehood.

Neither the ecstasy of becoming aware of a new, mysterious universe, nor the trauma and despair of being confronted with the magnitude of evil, impel clear thinking. Nevertheless, in ways one is apt to overlook as being clarifying, they do dislose the world and the human reality in striking and sobering ways. Moreover they restrain a readiness to impose the structures of our minds and perceptions upon realities being apprehended, temper the zeal for knowing and encourage one to become more deeply and sensitively aware: aware of this that cradles and fulfills our creaturehood, in minimal terms, The Creative Passage. It is minimal only as terminology. In reality it is all-encompassing and everlasting. Furthermore awareness of a new, mysterious universe and of the magnitude of human evil tends to disclose the role of clear thinking as being marginal in providing a perspective and the tools of thought with which to venture a working pattern of intelligibility and a disciplined appreciative awareness gives promise of a realistic stance of creaturehood.

Viewed within this context appreciative awareness becomes a highly existential notion, addressing our creaturehood, calling us back to the most elemental level of existing. Yet it presumes a discerning response rather than a collapse into an emotively geared piety. It presumes a disciplined outreach toward what may be "more than we can think," yet not beyond our awareness. In this respect the stance is comparable to that of aesthetics; and, in fact, is aesthetic in mode. The quotation which Dr. Mueller cites from Jane Dillenberger's *Secular Art with Sacred Themes* aptly depicts that stance:

> In making an analysis of painting or sculpture, we are compelled to verbalize that for which there is no verbal counterpart. Languages must be probing and pointing rather than definitive. Most important of all, the language must focus on the work of art itself, rather than on ideas about the work of art. It must compel the reader to become a viewer. p. 12.

x

Within any cosmology I would conceive of an appreciative consciousness as being relevant and informing. Within a format of reflection, however, that presupposes a mysterious universe, as in the new realism, it becomes imperative.

The religious reponse has always implied an interplay between familiar or manageable conceptualizations and the mysterious forces discerned in nature, or in what was conceived to be beyond nature; hence the affinities between the symbolisms of ritual or religious language and the occupational life of communities; or the affinities between the thought patterns of a people and their doctrinal expressions and creeds. Yet there has always attended this familiar base of knowable and intelligible patterns of meaning an outreach of wonder and awareness expressive of that sense of the Holy which could not be so encapsulated. Where that fringe of wonder and awareness has not been dissipated by too ready an enclosure within intelligible forms, the religious outreach has continued to be expressive imaginatively as well as expositionally or critically. The reverent, humble stance of a person, of whatever age or culture, acknowledging creaturehood, spans the centuries at the level of wonder, awareness and the appreciative response. Within specific cultures these assume a pattern distinctive of their tradition or aesthetic mode. It is important that this elemental human stance of creaturehood be acknowledged and respected wherever and however affirmed. There may arise need for more explicit designation of meaning, and a desire, even an insistence to explore it; but the integrity of creaturehood does not and cannot stand or fall on the definitively reasoned word. One has only to consult the legacy of discarded notions, premises or findings of Western thought within the spheres of theology, philosophy, or science to see that, though we had lived with them, we did not live by them. The enduring legacy inheres in the creatural outreach, itself; and what that evokes in a given time and place.

II.

Mueller may have reasons of his own for relating my use of the appreciative consciousness or appreciative awareness so explicitly to Liberalism. Insofar as the liberal ethos of thought was expressive of Kantian idealism, however, which in structural ways, elevated the moral consciousness, it veered from the mode of inquiry implied in appreciative awareness. What is more at stake in appreciative awareness is its orientation toward the relational datum in experience. The innovating turn of thought which awakened that kind of inquiry was William James' insistence that, contrary to Hume, "relations are experienceable and are experienced." This judgment was to prove influential in several directions after the turn of the century; notably in Husserl's mode of phenomenology, in Gestalt psychology, in Whitehead's philosophy of organism, and, implicitly, in contextualism. My own reflections in developing the notion of the appreciative consciousness are traceable in certain respects to the stimulus of both James and Whitehead: James in his insistence upon relations being experienceable, and Whitehead in his insistence upon viewing all order as being aesthetic order. In the latter, relations imply a textured or patterned way of envisaging individual and communal relations, as do relations between God and His creatures.

The import of the relational mode of envisagement as implied in appreciative awareness extends to all data of the environing universe: to wave particles as to all levels of creaturehood, countering the notion of mechanism; to temporal and spacial dimensions, as indicated in the imagery of space-time. That relational, yet individuated mode, occurring simultaneously, conveys integrity to individuated as to communal occurrences. And, in my use of this imagery, it becomes formative of insights concerning ultimacy within the immediacies of these lived experiences. It is this textured way of conceiving of the relational theme, as being individuated yet patterned, that lends distinctive import to the appreciative mode as expressed in appreciative awareness or the appreciative consciousness.

Mueller is correct in seeing this emphasis in my thought as being substantive in recovering an appeal to the traditional legacy, and in identifying it as being constituent of immediacies within both cultic and cultural as well as within individual experiences. And I concur with him in regarding this as a structural advance upon previous modes of liberal Christian thought; one that follows from resources I have employed in identifying the efficacy of the structure of experience. How one identifies what persists within the immediacies of experience by way of the structure of experience, however, can make a difference. In projecting the formula "doctrines are expendable, the legacy is not," I have weighted the structural continuity on the side of the cultural orbit of meaning which has given an historical and cultural shaping to the intention of meaning, both at the level of sensibility and of conceptualization. The explicit distillation of creedal judgment or doctrine within cultic expressions, influenced by philosophical, scientific, or other conceptualizing influences within any given period of history, may infuse too restrictive a vision of understanding upon that which is "more than we can think," or think adequately. Nevertheless, the impulse and intention of giving carrying power to the legacy within thought-forms meaningful and communicable within a given period of history is, as the modernists of the early Chicago School affirmed, important and impelling. I had always

xii

responded expectantly to the Chicago modernists' affirmation in this belief; yet could not see that they provided intellectual warrant for their claim, other than an implied biological imagery of genetic continuity, or their socio-historical confidence in Christianity as a social movement. By introducing the notion of the structure of experience, and informing it with insights drawn from Whitehead's interpretation of *causal efficacy*, I have felt that I strengthened this modernist appeal to an enduring and formative legacy within both cultus and culture; and, in varying degrees, within individual experiences as well.

In appealing to the legacy of faith, then, I am addressing covert dimensions of faith in contrast to overt procedures by which clarity of explicit, rational meaning is sought. It is commonplace to assume that in disciplined, rational or scientific procedures, distillations of clarity in meaning get to the truth of the matter. Seeking clarity or, perchance, simplicity may more properly be viewed as methodological procedures devised for purposes of rendering a body of data conceptually manageable; hence intelligible. The intent of my effort has been to view all such rationally clarified efforts functionally as a marginal overview within patterns of thought that are available and logically or scientifically persuasive. It may not follow, however, that the truth of the faith, or of the legacy, or more importantly, of Ultimacy as conveyed within these lived experiences, will have been captured or conveyed within these intelligible forms. Nevertheless, they may become, in the words of Ian Ramsey, "disclosure models" for generating further inquiry.

The inter-relating of these two disciplined modes of inquiry: one bent on open awareness, the other on a tentative effort of enclosure within a manageable system of intelligible forms, is not readily achieved; hence the effort to relate them is readily rejected. Instead it may be urged that both be available, but not inter-related. The need to relate them has seemed to me to be so urgent and possibly rewarding, that I have been impelled to pursue the interchange despite the difficulties entailed.

One of the major difficulties incurred in such a procedure is that of language. One rhythm of inquiry is bent on addressing the import and character of open awareness; the other on being expressive within a manageable system of terms. Dr. Mueller comments on the problem of language in my discourse and offers various explanations to account for it. Strangely, however, he omits this one which is integral to the method of inquiry I pursue, entailing the effort to relate the appreciative and the definitively rational modes.

III.

In identifying the orientaton of my thought theologically, Dr. Mueller suggests that my stance be seen as having moved beyond and away from liberalism. I can understand his having come to that judgment, for in all three volumes of the trilogy I speak critically of liberalism, often without characterizing or identifying the mode of liberalism being criticized. In addressing historical forms of liberal Christian thought, commonly referred to as Rationalism, Romanticism, and Modernism, I have identified Liberalism as the generic term, implying that these other terms designate three historical cycles within that modern movement. Recently I have ventured to suggest that one might look upon various contemporary movements of theological expression, movements commonly referred to as "post-liberal" or "post-modern," as having initiated a fourth cycle of Liberalism. I imply this obliquely in *Fallible Forms and Symbols* in speaking of certain phenomenologically, existentialist, and process oriented modes of religious inquiry partaking of the mood of new realism. Thus, however critical I may be toward former cycles of Liberalism, or of strands within the contemporary cycle, such judgments are not to be understood as implying departure from the essential, historical thrust of the liberal ethos. The distinction between liberalism and traditionalism, or liberalism and orthodoxy is not really at issue here. What is at issue is historical identity and continuity within the Judaic-Christian legacy. Each of the earlier cycles provided tenuous grounds for asserting such continuity, though the thrust of inquiry in each instance was to stress the innovating lure of contemporaneity. To be sure the innovating lure has been no less assertive within the more current, Existentialist Cycle; yet its facilities of thought provide it with resources and motivation which are substantive and imaginative in restating the grounds informing such cultural and cultic continuity. My own efforts within this latter cycle of Liberalism, drawing upon resources provided within the new vision of science and of process thought, have given particular attention to vivifying the structural continuities. Mueller is correct in seeing this latter emphasis in my thought as being substantive in recovering an appeal to the traditional legacy, and in identifying it as being constituent of immediacies within both cult and culture. And I concur with him in regarding it as a structural advance upon previous modes of liberal, Christian thought—one that follows from resources I have employed in identifying the efficacy of the structure of experience.

How one identifies what persists within the immediacies of experience by way of that structure, however, can make a difference. In projecting the formula, "doctrines are expendable; the legacy is not," I have weighted the structural continuity on the side of the orbit of meaning, which has given an historical shaping and intention of meaning, both at the level of sensibility and symbolization. The explicit distillations of creedal judgment and doctrinal formulations, influenced by philosophical, scientific, or other tentatively held cultural conceptualizations within a given period of history, may impose too restrictive or temporally conditioned vision of understanding upon "that which is more than we can think" or think adequately, to be continuously informing or instructive. This qualification would apply to every period of history. Conceivably the symbolisms implicit in doctrine may be retained in liturgy and art, where the intent is to affirm or to celebrate the historical continuity of faith. In that context, historical doctrines tend to become assimilated to the legacy of faith, and need no longer bear the burden of explicit, literal meaning.

A serious and disciplined response to one's thought becomes in itself a testament to attend for its own sake and on its own terms. Dr. Mueller's contribution in this vein lies in focusing concern on what he understands to be the import of my work for imparting or communicating Christian faith within the contemporary Church. He sees that constructive import stemming from three areas: (1) *the appreciative* consciousness as a mode of religious response and inquiry illumining the stimulus and nurture of the creatural outreach; (2) the relation of the legacy of faith to *the cultural orbit of meaning;* and (3) the symbolism of *the structure of experience* as providing a living nexus of inherited symbolism and imagery. These he projects as resources of insight informing Christian faith within the contemporary witness of the Church. I am grateful for these efforts and expectations.

Bernard E. Meland

PREFACE

I have continually been amazed at people's ability to recall "firsts" in their lives: whether the first meeting of someone, the first step toward a decision, or the first time something was tried. Many PREFACES narrate the first reading of a book, or an introductory encounter with a person, or the initial inspiration from which a work grew. My life is no exception. After writing this dissertation and investigating the turns of my own mind over the years that brought me here, I recall many "firsts." Only two of these merit mentioning here. I recall my first introduction to "process" thought in Whitehead's *Religion in the Making*. It was assigned reading in a philosophy of God course that I took at St. Louis University. The experience that remains indelibly in my memory is akin to a sailor at sea, surely on the brink of being swamped by the waves of "concrescences" and "epochal occasions." It seemed a strange and shifting world of thought. Many years later, and many journeys more through such people as Whitehead, the feeling has changed. The feeling is rather that of an experienced seaman who knows the dangers of the sea, respects it, and yet welcomes the chance to set sail again because the sea is a friend. "Process" thought has enriched my own development.

The second "first" was my first acquaintance with Bernard E. Meland through the pages of *The Future of Empirical Theology* (1969). In the spirit of a graduate seminar that I was taking at Graduate Theological Union (GTU), it was "recommended" reading. Ironically, the course was taught by the same man who knew Meland at the University of Chicago in 1945—Bernard Loomer. I was impressed by Meland's article on the history of the Chicago School. In it, Meland showed himself honest and insightful to the development of the American scene. It was clear that he had a privileged historical position with many of the trends that had become powerful movements in American thought. More reading of Meland's works gradually uncovered another source to "process" thought with which Whitehead had been associated. But this is many journeys later, after my initial reading of Whitehead, and I had become more secure at sea. Meland offered this alternative to me: passage on a theological ship. Meland's ports of faith, culture, myth, secularization, consciousness, Jesus Christ, the Spirit, and God were more appealing. I thought that perhaps I had found an excursion ship by which I could investigate and then chart my own course. I like the way Robert Frost said it in "The Road Not Taken."

Yet knowing how way leads on to way,
I doubted if I should ever come back.

I shall be telling this with a sigh
Somewhere ages and ages hence:

Two roads diverged in a wood, and I—
I took the one less traveled by,
And that has made all the difference.

Though not all the reasons for choosing a topic are necessarily clear or articulated, some central reasons recur around which all other reasons seem to cluster. One central reason is the fact that Meland is a theologian.

Bernard E. Meland (1899—   ) was professor of the Constructive Theology department at the Divinity School of the University of Chicago from 1946 until his retirement in 1964. An alumnus of the Divinity School (1929), Meland taught at Central College (Fayette, Missouri) and Pomona College (Claremont, California). Since his retirement, he has lived close to the University of Chicago.[1] Trained in the empirical methodology of the University of Chicago, Meland remained open to the developments in philosophy, cultural anthropology, psychology, and literature. In what became known as "process" thought in philosophy, which began with William James and was singularly represented by Alfred North Whitehead, Meland drew upon their insights for a new perception of theological inquiry. Whereas many thinkers move toward a philosophy of God in the manner of Whitehead and Hartshorne, Meland retains his theological identity.[2] The question becomes one of theological concern with "process" thought. Meland's work is the most complete, systematized, and original theological representation. This representation comes in what he calls his trilogy: *Faith and Culture* (1953), *The Realities of Faith: The Revolution in Cultural Forms* (1962), and *Fallible Forms and Symbols: Discourses on Method for a Theology of Culture* (1976). Together, they represent a theology of culture.

Meland brings other qualities to his trilogy. As an active theologian throughout the period of many revolutionary cultural and scientific developments that have catapulted our world into a new era, he represents a unique glimpse into this historical development. For this position alone, Meland would be worth investigation.

Meland brings an historical perspective that appreciates the need for tradition. In a changing world, identity is a problem. These "fallible forms" raise the question of what is constitutive and what is contingent. Although Meland has no easy answer, his willingness to grapple with the Christian tradition and make it a constitutive part of his theologizing is important. In the wake of what was symbolized in the Catholic Church at Vatican II (1963-65), there was a growing acknowledgement of the cultural influences, intellectual patterns and presuppositions, and historically unique developments that needed intensive attention. Even the simple adjective "American" changes and specifies the identity or lack of it of all the above.[3] A responsibility to those influences that are impinging upon the American Christian has to be accepted. Meland offers one access that is not only historically important but has also a prophetic quality operative today. Meland related to me that it is interesting to him that what seemed difficult to graduate students who read his *Faith and Culture* in 1954 and found it bewildering has given way to undergraduate college students today reading and understanding it with enthusiasm.[4] What gives this character of speaking ahead of one's time is not clear. Certainly reasons could be marshalled. Unmistakably, however, is a quality of perception, expression, and truth that is worth study.

Meland brings one other dimension to his trilogy which is the Appreciative Consciousness. David Tracy and others have pointed out that in today's pluralism there is need for some philosophical basis for a truth claim that is made by an author.[5] In other words, people must be allowed to travel that road with the author to see what he has seen. Meland has presented an experiential American approach to theology with an emphasis upon the total person: emotional, affective, moral, and intellectual.[6] Meland's main thrust is the recognition of the "appreciative" dimension in consciousness along with the rational and moral dimensions. In other words, Meland tries to bring a complete understanding of the human person in relation to a theology of culture. Most specifically, he does his theology of culture through an examination of the faith of the individual in the cultural context and relationships that are part and parcel of human living. What qualitatively occurs is a new way of doing theology.

In a review of *Fallible Forms and Symbols*, David L. Hall in 1978 makes the important statement: "Tarred or whitewashed. . . with the same brush as other 'Chicago Theologians,' he [Meland] has been both praised and dismissed as one of the proponents of the post-liberal tradition in theology. I believe we need fewer considerations of Meland's thinking which situate and articulate his 'place in contemporary theology' and more discussions of his importance as a thinker capable of making significant contributions to the issue of the relations of religious sensibility to culture."[7] I totally agree. My work is precisely a step in that direction.

I was surprised that although critics and reviewers of Meland admit the importance of the Appreciative Awareness, relatively little has been done on it. Even more wanting is the relationship of the Appreciative Consciousness to faith. As I read and worked on Meland, I came to maintain that one cannot fully understand Meland's concept of faith without understanding his Appreciative Consciousness. To take this one step further, which speaks to the complaint of "complexity" readers first have with Meland, his work on culture, secularization, myth, and the use of tradition all radiate outwards from his central theme of Faith and its relationship to the Appreciative mode. My work is an attempt to penetrate and express this central and fruitful insight. My method will be to proceed to Meland's central theme of Faith through his concept of the Appreciative Awareness (Ch. 1). Together, they form the leverage for his theology of culture. Appreciative Awareness comes from a background of Liberal theology (Intro.) as a reply to a deficiency in that Liberal tradition. The deficiency is most clearly detected in the change in root imagery. Appreciative Awareness is the conscious, vectoral perception that yields knowledge in the form of wonder, hunches, musements, and intuitions. It is closely akin to the aesthetic appreciation expressed in artistic endeavors and skills. But, although it began for Meland in art, especially in music, and his own appreciation, it is wider, deeper, and more pervasive than artistic appreciation. Appreciative for Meland convokes the "textured character" of all living and reality. The emphasis is relational-contextual.

Whereas Appreciative Awareness is a skill that can be developed, Faith is a gift. The definition of faith (Ch. 2) will be juxtaposed to the Appreciative Awareness. The context of Faith will be pointed out which comes through the Individual, the Culture, and the Cultus (Ch. 3). Having given the context of his theology, the content will follow. I selected the central Christian mystery of the Trinity as an organizing unit: the revelation of God, Jesus Christ, and the Holy Spirit (Ch. 4). Finally, it will be possible to present the Appreciative Awareness and Faith in their precise relationship (Ch. 5). Finally, some further considerations will follow as indication of possible development of Meland's thought. For the convenience of the reader, and for the advantage of a clearer presentation, I have included a glossary of Meland's principal terms.

Upon reflection, my work has had to make several original forays into Meland's works. One was the use of the trilogy in its completed form. A second was a study of the development of the Appreciative Awareness. A third was the presentation of Meland's understanding of Faith as the central theme of the trilogy. The fourth was the relationship of Faith and the Appreciative Awareness which is the topic itself. A fifth was the relationship of Faith and Appreciative Awareness to Meland's empirical understanding of the trinity.

Throughout Meland's works, I became sensitized to the imagery that he uses and his critique of imagery in cultural thought. One particular image that is relevant here is his description of fire. He says that fire will not be confined by the structures containing it. Sooner or later, the fire will inevitably consume the structure and break into the open. I would conclude my preface here by saying that the image is much like Meland himself. His work will not be contained, nor will his spirit. I hope that in my work I can help fan the flames.

NOTES

[1] Meland has just released a number of autobiographical accounts of himself which may be found at the University of Chicago or the Process Center in Claremont, California.

[2] There seem to be two distinct approaches in "process" thought: one is ontological and the other is empirical. Whitehead and Hartshorne belong to the ontological side and consider themselves philosophers. I believe Ogden and Cobb also belong to this side although some exception might be taken in the case of Cobb. On the other side, Loomer, D.D. Williams, Meland, and more recently, Bernard Lee belong to this empirical side. Interestingly, this empirical cluster all consider themselves theologians. Two recent theologians who begin from experience are David Tracy and Donald Gelpi, Tracy moving to the ontological and Gelpi the empirical side.

[3] The studies of American Catholicism can be adequately found in John Tracy Ellis, *American Catholicism* (Chicago: University of Chicago, 1969), and Thomas T. McAvoy, *A History of the Catholic Church in the U.S.*, Notre Dame: University of Notre Dame Press, 1969).

[4] This statement came from Meland himself in an interview that I had with him in November, 1978. Meland also spoke of the publisher's receipts that had been forwarded to him of copies of his books sold. The number had increased recently.

[5] David Tracy, *Blessed Rage for Order* (New York: Seabury, 1975).

[6] There is a need today to investigate the entire person's involvement in faith. Two such efforts along this line that are important and helpful are Bernard Lonergan's *Method in Theology* (New York: Herder & Herder, 1972), and Donald Gelpi's *Experiencing God* (New York: Paulist Press, 1978). Both of these speak about the conversion process from a total human approach.

[7] David Hall's critical review of Meland's *Fallible Forms and Symbols*, Process Studies, Vol. 7, No. 2, 1978, p. 112.

INTRODUCTION

The Background of Meland's Theologizing

What I proposed to do in this introduction is present Meland's reaction to the form of thought that had immediately preceded him which he labels "Liberalism." Liberalism is undermined by the change in imagery as the Western world shifted to atomic theories and new understandings of power. The new imagery is the pivot away from Liberalism and toward renewed resources of faith.

Liberalism

The expression which describes the historical background against which Bernard E. Meland does his theologizing is "Liberalism" which can also be expressed as the "Liberal Era." This background of theological Liberalism reflects the intellectual development of Protestantism in its liberal phase. Meland's concern for liberal Protestantism also includes the contours which delineate the liberal movement. This means that the conservative Protestant thrust also partakes of the Liberal heritage but as something to be fled or ignored. With a few variations, it would be true of Catholicism in Europe and America.

For the sake of clarity, Meland designates the Liberal Era as the period between Descartes and Barth. He describes it as a three-staged development. The first stage begins with the age of Enlightenment, symbolized in Descartes, which had a new appreciation for the power and role of reason. Reason challenged the role and authority of divine revelation. Reason began to displace the notion of revelation as the source of confidence. The second stage begins with Kant and his elevation of moral faith to dominance. Reason alone did not give confidence. Faith, as opposed to reason, asserted its own position of confidence toward reality. Religious and moral ideals asserted a more independent position which displaced the notion of redemption as a divine act alone. The third and final stage emphasized experience as the controlling concept of confidence in all modes of inquiry. One result was that the psychological study of religion received impetus and expanded conventionally understood theological doctrines such that they became subject to interpretation through their psychological meaningfulness. Certainly the pioneer work of the Father of Psychiatry, Freud, is such an instance.[1]

Meland does go into detail in other places for specific reference to this Liberal Era. Meland includes pragmatic liberals and modernists of the early Chicago school, Continental and American Ritschlians, personalists, and religious humanists.[2] These theologies all share the imagery and fundamental notions of idealism, either in the form of moral idealism in which "self-experience" was made normative (Ritschlianism, personalism, religious humanism), or of a conceptualism or conceptual theism (the Chicago school of Shailer Mathews and Edward Scribner Ames).[3] In another place, Meland tells us why pragmatism falls into this appraisal, especially as a "truncated Idealism":

> The focus of interest in Pragmatism, as in Hebraicism and in Calvinism, however, is so strenuously upon the *work of men* together that the recognition of deeper initiation of meaning is held within the bounds of these observable historical events, i.e., 'men working and communing together.'

> Pragmatism is a kind of secularized account of this theme of men working and communing together, informed by the sciences and by romanticist expectations of man. It is thus awakened to the promise of this corporate fact of men working and communing together in a way that Calvinism never could be.[4]

The one exception for Meland is Schleiermacher. He was able to convey in his notion of "absolute dependence" the sense of "otherness" that seemed to escape the enclosures of both intellectualism and moralism.[5]

Karl Barth is the end-point of the Liberal Era. He symbolizes the Neo-Orthodoxy line of protest against Liberalism. Neo-Orthodoxy, however, does not neatly separate Liberalism from Post-Liberal theology. Neo-Orthodoxy really belongs to the Liberal Era in imagery even though it protests the Liberal Era. In other words, Neo-Orthodoxy never managed to remove itself from the Liberal heritage in order to provide a critical stance apart from Liberalism. In short, it was a defensive Liberalism.[6] The line of protest that it made did call for a new realism but it remained helpless to provide that realism. Interestingly enough, and perhaps confirming Meland's appraisal, the New Realism emerged around 1945 and Neo-Orthodoxy desisted.[7]

The search for a new realism echoed in the problem of language. Recovery of Christian words proved to be a stumbling block to the Liberal movement. Neo-Orthodoxy benefited from such other sources as the sociological use of Christian words through the American philosopher Josiah Royce; such as, atonement, grace, judgment, sin, redemption, and loyalty.[8] Tradition took on new meaning. The Liberals had no other word for what was happening than to call it a return to orthodoxy, or "neo-orthodoxy." But this was guilt by association for the new protest and a reluctance on the part

2

of Liberalism to inquire into the revolution in conceptual forms that was taking place in the sciences, philosophy, and even theology.[9] New life and new energies searched for understanding and expression. A frontier of new realism was emerging, "breaking free of the enclosure of mentalism which had engulfed philosophical thinking in the West for more than three hundred years and which had shaped the imagery of theological liberalism since the time of Kant."[10]

What then is the Liberal spirit which Neo-Orthodoxy protested and Meland appraises? The liberal spirit employs the findings of the sciences as a way to illumine faith within the idiom of modern culture and thus transmit its teaching more readily to others through the persuasion of the sciences.[11] In other words, the meaningfulness of faith comes from science. Liberal Christianity therefore refuses to equate science with secularism which is the tendency to exclude any need for God or the transcendent. Scientific understanding really aids self-understanding. But what occurs finally is that scientific inquiry supplants theological inquiry. Any tension between science and faith was abrogated in favor of uniformity. As such, though Liberal theologians were in a favored positon to note cultural depths and the pervasiveness of the Judaic-Christian faith in the Western experience so alive at the time, most by-passed this interest completely. Such a blind spot is not easily explained. Meland attributes it to the "studied avoidance" of mythical and imaginative dimensions which simply were not of interest. The suppression of the imaginative dimension certainly continued due to the insufficiency of the philosophical imagery and concepts, especially the lack of organic and contextual imagery.[12] The imagery that did dominate the strategies of thought in Liberalism was "self-experience." It was as if the climate of self enveloped the whole of the experiential world.[13] As such, the Liberal Era offered little occasion of real encounter with realities other than self. The self was the center of being from which one ventured outward like Don Quixote and colored and shaped that world by the individual ego or whatever the mind would allow. The result was that there was no dimension of good beyond or outside the human reason or moral good. Communities were simply collections of individuals. It was a one-way street of unilateral relationships.

The "controlling metaphor" of the age[14] was Newtonian Mechanics. Basically Newtonian science rejects any assumption that the realities of existence might elude the forms of human thought. The universe is ordered and yields to correct and logical reasoning whether in the form of equations or causes. Euclidean geometry, for instance, expressed reality "as it really is." Its clarity and obviousness did not necessitate questioning it as a mathematical presupposition. The paradigmatic imagery upon which thinking rests is the perspective that nature works in such a mechanistic parallel that it truly yields to mathematics. Thus, the power of observation and description, combined with reason, yielded the nuggets of existence. A.N. Whitehead presents this perspective in physics when he so poignantly recalls,

> When I went up to Cambridge early in the 1880's my ma-
> thematical training was continued under good teachers.
> Now nearly everything was supposed to be known about
> physics that could be known—except a few spots, such as
> electromagnetic phenomena, which remained (or so it
> was thought) to be co-ordinated with the Newtonian
> principles. But, for the rest, physics was supposed to be
> nearly a closed subject. Those investigations to co-ordin-
> ate went on through the next dozen years. By the middle
> of the 1890's there were a few tremors, a slight shiver as
> of all not being quite secure, but no one sensed what was
> coming. By 1900 Newtonian physics were demolished,
> done for! Speaking personally, it had a profound effect
> on me; I have been fooled once, and I'll be damned if I'll
> be fooled again.[15]

Meaningfulness does not necessarily yield truth. And clarity is not necessarily the indicator of meaning. Newtonian mechanics bowed out to a newer realism.

This background of Liberalism is most important for Meland's theologizing. The present understanding of theology continues to draw strength from what has gone before, whether for good or bad. It is similar to the person who must accept both the good experiences of the past as well as the bad experiences in order to come to a realistic self-knowledge. A re-appropriation of the energies of these three hundred years must be recovered, not lost. Meland here acknowledges the cultural and intellectual energies rooted in the past. The Christian Liberal leaned upon Newtonian imagery to illumine the Christian faith. The Post-Liberal Christian will rely upon some other imagery, but this need not exclude the contributions that the human community made while drawing upon that imagery. This also means that newer imagery will possess a power to explain and to illumine faith in a way that the older imagery could not. The topic of Liberalism has not been ex-hausted with this brief treatment, it will emerge over and over again in Meland's thought and the direction he takes when he has a choice. One such choice will be his development of the Appreciative Awareness. As Meland ex-plains the function of the Appreciative Awareness and Faith:

> This is the reverse of demythologizing. It is recovering
> what the liberal era forfeited: namely, a vivid sense of
> this shaping and redemptive force to which the life of
> faith bears witness as an elemental, creatureal response.

This, in my judgment, is not going back to liberalism but through it and beyond it, repossessing on critical grounds what liberal disciplines helped to establish, the witness of faith expressive of the mythos which persists with efficacy, informing and motivating our structure of experience.[16]

The New Imagery

Newtonian Mechanics provided the basic imagery for Liberalism. A revolution in imagery would mean a swift and unexpected transition of the undergirdings of thought. The effects might take the form of a slow decay to Liberalism rather than a shattering blow. Neo-Orthdoxy protested Liberalism but did not attend to the basic imagery that underwent a revolution. As such Neo-Orthodoxy battled the tip of the iceberg, while itself depending on what remained below the surface. Only the revolution in newer imagery awaited timely birth and maturer development. Meland traces this development and its revolution of imagery into the Age of Power.

A whole series of discoveries took place in the physical sciences which heralded the change from Newtonian Mechanics to the Age of Power. Though many influences can be traced which contributed to the newer imagery, the first clear discovery which belongs to the new age is 1895 when Roentgen discovered the X-ray.[17] Then a revolution in the conception of the atom occurred about 1896 when Becquerel and the Curies discovered radioactive elements. These discoveries set in motion a whole chain of discoveries that led to the reformulation of physics which was labeled accordingly, "the new vision of science."[18] Just after the turn of the century, Rutherford discovered the proton with the disclosure that the atom is planetary in character. The Newtonian-Cartesian age was irremediably and dramatically severed from the new vision of science.

In other areas, the revolution in imagery remained relatively unknown. Gradually, inroads were made. In 1924, Meland himself remembers the puzzled faculty at the University of Chicago when Henry Nelson Wieman was invited to explain to the faculty the bewildering writings of Alfred North Whitehead. As Meland himself describes the gradual maturation of this newer imagery:

Suddenly scholars, insofar as they were susceptible to scientific influence, broke out with the markings of field theory and other holistic notions. Relativity was in all this too. The theory had been set forth by Einstein in 1905, although it was not until Heisenberg announced

5

the principle of indeterminacy in 1931 that these new theories in physics, relativity and quantum mechanics, assumed wide currency outside scientific discussions and highly technical philosophical speculations. Not until 1945, however, with the falling of atomic bombs on Hiroshima and Nagasake, did all this revolution in imagery become a public fact. Thus the age of atomic power did not burst upon us out of the blue. Its antecedents can be fully studied. They had been widely known throughout scientific and industrial circles before the turn of the century.[19]

The new imagery unveils a shift in consciousness. If the imagery of Newtonian science rejects the assumption that the realities of existence elude the forms of human thought, the so-called "new" imagery acknowledges the mystery and indeterminacy of human thought. The new imagery which includes its method of science recognizes the discontinuity between the clarity of thought and the reality it claims to portray. Meland has a favorite expression for this discrepancy: the "manageable" and "unmanageable" aspects of events. The "manageable" refers to what can be made clear, but it cannot go to such an extent as to claim a one-to-one correspondence to truth. The "unmanageable" refers to what cannot be clearly and completely described. The fuzziness and ambiguity of reality which does not yield to human thought has just as much a claim for truth.[20] What the "manageable" and "unmanageable" indicate is the "dimension of depth" in reality. "Depth" means "that the realities of any experience are to be accounted deeper than, or in some aspects resistant to, man's powers of observation and description."[21] This is not a rejection of the power of reason, but a recognition of its limits. The cognitive expression which accounts for this depth will require Meland's attention and it will result in his development of the Appreciative Awareness. Before moving to the Appreciative Awareness, important developments in the change of imagery still have to be attended to.

Scientific Convergences

Not only in the area of the new physics, but in the other sciences also, the new vision subverted, then dominated and controlled, the conceptual arena. The particular change that Meland indicates in imagery can be exemplified in biology and its theory of evolution. The early and remarkable theories of evolution by Darwin and Spencer belong to Newtonian imagery for they did not break away from this basis. It was Newtonian mechanics which undergirded evolution and allowed the discovery. In other words, Newtonian mechanics was the nurturing matrix for evolutionary theory. Even though the theory of evolution contributed to the newer realism that was to follow, it was not until the "Emergent evolutionists" like Lloyd Morgan, Jan Smuts, and S. Alexander that Newtonian mechanical selection yielded to an organic approach.[22] This movement has sometimes been referred to as "organicism." Their insight probed the interrelationship of emergence and structure. Both work together to sustain life and allow for novelty in selection. Though these philosopher-biologists from the British school never managed to have any one of their group present a completely convincing case, nevertheless as a whole much of their imagery and insight remains in the new realism as premises accepted in other sciences.

The new behavioral sciences developed along with the new imagery and made their own contributions to it. In cultural anthropology, a more sensitive outreach of the human person as related to culture opened up a wholeness of personality within the context of culture. There was an organic relationship of the individual to culture. Individual forms of expression solidified in cultural expressions. The function and formation of myth became key to both the individual and culture. Myth is educative for future generations and a rallying point of identity for tribes, nations, and cultures. Intellectual premises and processes partake of the same fabric and texture of culture as well. In fact, the importance of culture cannot be ignored as a formative ground for valuations that even reach the innermost center of the human psyche. Hence, the contextual character of human living from myth, ritual, emotions, and concepts present the newer realism in its past and present as inextricably cultural.

Drawing upon cultural anthropology and its insights of contextual wholeness, psychology developed new methods of examining the human person. "Gestalt" psychology emerged about 1925 as well as Field Theory which emphasizes the individual and the context.[23] Behaviorism as mechanistic and solely causal gradually yielded to a complex of feeling responses in which, on the positive side, motives, incentives, and aspirations were generated by the individual; or, on the negative side, responses in which blockages, resentments, and psychical defeat occur which hinder the personal development. The view of the psychophysical organic relationship is not a subjectivism but a deepened appraisal of the human person beyond mechanism. Developmental psychology emerged and presented the person as a *human* person with *human* responses not entirely clear or circumscribed by coherent models. Overall, psychology attended to the new realism with its examination of interrelationships, contexts, development, creativity, and growth of the individual.

In Philosophy, a new metaphysics sought faithfully to generalize the categories that had become elaborated and persuasive in the new vision of science. Previously, the philosophy of Kant had held sway. In Meland's judgment, Protestantism had found its "Thomas Aquinas," so influential was Kant to Protestant theology.[24] Kant emphasized the rational and moral dimension of thought characteristic of Liberalism. The moral measure of value and the moral concern about the individual dominated religious inquiry since reason alone could not explain the motivation for choices that were made. Moral consciousness competed with rational consciousness. Kant was seen to have presented a rational justification for the Reformation's appeal to faith expressed by Martin Luther.[25] Not until Henri Bergson and William James is the metaphysical question of the individual in relation to all reality given a different perspective philosophically. Both of these men challenged Kant's presuppositions and revolutionized the metaphysical perception. The theory of "duration" in Bergson and that of "Internal Relations" in James opened up a new appropriation of the human person. The most comprehensive metaphysical expression of this thrust was that of Alfred North Whitehead. This "philosophy of organism" as Whitehead labeled it is the most marked example and radical summation of the dimension of the philosophical shift from Newtonian mechanics to an atomistic world-view of the new realism.

Though other disciplines could also serve to present the transition to the newer imagery, Meland borrows insights from these for his theology. The important point is that these disciplines converge on their agreement of a more complex and elusive notion of reality than Newtonian mechanics with its measureable and describable presupposition of reality.[26] Ian Ramsey has a famous shorthand formula to present this change in imagery: "picture models" and "disclosure models."[27] The "picture model" is the mode of thinking within the era of Newtonian science which assumed that scientific discoveries progressively and ineluctably contributed to a total picture of the natural order. The sum of the sciences added even more to the total picture of nature as a whole. The "disclosure model" is the Post-Newtonian model and presents discoveries as intermittent, where many attempts are made but only a few succeed. Newtonian science thereby yields a clear picture of reality; the post-Newtonian science yields only a partial disclosure of a complex and mysterious reality. In the disclosure model, "every act of inquiry, scientific, philosophical, or religious, presupposing coherence on a cosmic scale, or the notion of order as an ultimate picture of reality, is asserted as an act of faith, not as a proven fact of science or philosophy."[28] This religious dimension of the new imagery opens an interesting perspective on the role of faith as a disclosure of reality which Meland explores and exploits. It is enough now to indicate that faith's roots spread throughout the fundamental scientific imagery.

Between Background and Foreground

Meland is no stranger to either the Liberal Era or the Age of Power. Trained at the University of Chicago and receiving his degree in 1929, he was educated within the control of the Liberal Era. His own acceptance of a position on the faculty of the University of Chicago coincided with the "public

8

fact" of the revolution of Atomic imagery.[29] The first volume of his three-volumed theology of culture came out in 1953 and wrestled with insights of the new imagery upon Faith. The trilogy itself signaled a change in Meland's theologizing. From the perspective of the newer imagery, the background of Liberalism can be critiqued for its inadequacies. In the same way, an honest appraisal of the background serves to illuminate the foreground of the new imagery and to set apart its energies. One such example is the Appreciative Awareness which Meland develops from the inadequacies of the Liberal Era and which will become instrumental for the act of faith.

NOTES

INTRODUCTION

[1] Bernard E. Meland, *Fallible Forms and Symbols: Discourses on Method for a Theology of Culture* (Philadelphia: Fortress Press, 1976), p. 16. (Hereafter cited as FFS.)

[2] Ibid., p. 9.

[3] Meland is the best historian of the Chicago School. See his article on "The Empirical Tradition in Theology at Chicago," *The Future of Empirical Theology*, ed. Bernard Meland (Chicago: University of Chicago Press, 1969), 283-306.

[4] Bernard E. Meland, "A Post-Retreat Comment to Professor Haroutunian," *Criterion* (Winter, 1964), p. 12.

[5] FFS, p. 9. Along with Schleiermacher, Meland sees Otto and Tillich in this line because of their appeal to the *numinis*.

[6] Ibid., p. 6.

[7] One of the best historians of Neo-Orthodoxy is Sidney Ahlstrom: *A Religious History of the American People* (New Haven: Yale, 1972); and *Theology in America*, ed. (New York: Bobbs-Merrill Co., Inc., 1967).

[8] FFS, p. 7. For Josiah Royce, see his *The Problem of Christianity* (2 vols., Chicago: Regnery, 1968).

[9] Ibid., pp. 7-8.

[10] Ibid., p. 5.

[11] Bernard E. Meland, *The Realities of Faith: The Revolution in Cultural Forms* (New York: Oxford University Press, 1962; paperback, Chicago: Seminary Cooperative Bookstore, 1970) (hereafter cited as RF.)

10

[12] FFS, pp. 86—7.

[13] RF, p. 197.

[14] Ian Barbour, *Myths, Models and Paradigms* (New York: Harper, 1974).

[15] RF, p. 145; or Lucien Price, *Dialogues of Alfred North Whitehead*, (Mentor, 1956), p. 277.

[16] FFS, p. 143.

[17] RF, p. 91.

[18] FFS, p. 26.

[19] RF, p. 92.

[20] Ibid., p. 93.

[21] Ibid.

[22] Bernard E. Meland, *Faith and Culture* (New York: Oxford University Press, 1953), p. 8. (Hereafter cited as FC.)

[23] Eisendrath quotes Victor Lowe's developments that influenced Whitehead: "the development of vector physics, the development of the theories of molecular and submolecular energetic vibration, and thirdly the rise of field as a basic concept. Later come the statistical conception of physical laws, the theory of relativity, and the quantum theory." p. xi. Craig Eisendrath says that of these developments, the most important were probably vector physics and field theory. p. 241, n. 9. Craig Eisendrath, *The Unifying Moment: The Psychological Philosophy of William James and Alfred North Whitehead* (Cambridge: Harvard University Press, 1971). Meland also has a statement of Field Theory in RF, p. 257.

[24] Bernard E. Meland, *Higher Education and the Human Spirit* (Chicago: University of Chicago Press, 1963; paperback, Chicago: Seminary Cooperative Bookstore, 1965), p. 49. (Hereafter cited as HEHS.)

[25] Ibid., p. 49.

[26] FFS, p. 26.

[27] Ibid., p. 26, n. 4.

[28] Ibid., p. 26.

[29] This "public fact" was the atomic bomb and its use upon Japan.

THE APPRECIATIVE AWARENESS

In this chapter, I will present Bernard E. Meland's concept of the Appreciative Awareness. The Appreciative Awareness has its roots in the Liberalism and change in imagery mentioned in the introduction. I will present the history of its development in Meland's thought. Since it is not specifically a religious concept, but a cognitive one, I will explain the sources of its formation in Bergson, James, and Whitehead. Its application to religious thought then becomes possible, both with its danger of subjectivism and its corrective method which is one of the unique contributions of this epistemology to its religious dimension.

The History of Appreciative Awareness

The concept of the Appreciative Awareness develops out of the background of the Liberal Era. The inadequacy of the paradigmatic imagery which pervaded most forms of inquiry shifted such that a newer imagery replaced the older one. The act of inquiry in the individual settled upon the rational and moral consciousness. In other words, reason measured reality or else the will did through what was good or bad even if reason did not agree. Sometimes, as Kant saw, the moral choice stood in contrast to reason. Certainly faith and reason were antinomies. But in the newer imagery, experience becomes more important in the sense that it must be taken seriously and a more complete notion of experience must be examined. This is not self-experience moving outward from the individual, but a contextual and relational understanding of experience in mutual interaction. To put it another way, reality in many forms outside of the individual asserts itself which has nothing to do with self-assertion. To capture this dimension of experience as an integral part of consciousness along with the rational and moral realms, Meland develops the Appreciative Consciousness. Together, the Rational, Moral, and Appreciative forms of consciousness apprehend the "New Realism" of the Age of Power.

The Appreciative Awareness is not unique to Meland in that it is an aesthetic mode of thinking. He refers to Henry Nelson Wieman's use of it, for instance. What is unique to Meland is his description, explanation, and use of it. Meland uses the concept of Appreciative Awareness in his first book in 1934, *Modern Man's Worship*. Not until 1953 in his book *Higher Education and the Human Spirit* does Meland explicitly discuss the concept itself. This book represents his reflections back upon his educational experience in

Fayette, Missouri, and Pomona College in Claremont, California, teaching mostly the history and philosophy of religion. In 1945, Meland accepted the position at the Divinity School at the University of Chicago in Constructive Theology. The momentous events of World War II, the atomic bomb, the news of concentration camps and exterminations, focused his attention in his new postion to theologize concerning those traumatic and perilous times.[1] A shift in Meland's theologizing occurred.[2] Intimations of the transition appeared in his two books *Seeds of Redemption* (1947) and *The Reawakening of Christian Faith* (1949) which were a series of public lectures given in the early 1940's. Constructive Theology implies "a focusing of theological interest upon immediate demands and concerns of living as these evoke and convey the realities of faith."[3] The assumption is that faith is a vital response and not a legacy of belief from the past. Since the dynamics of the lived experience involve many relationships, constructive theology assumes proportions of a theology of culture. Simultaneously with *Higher Education and the Human Spirit* (1953), Meland published the first volume of his trilogy *Faith and Culture* (1953). The other two are *The Realities of Faith* (1962) and *Fallible Forms and Symbols* (1976). Meland's concept of the Appreciative Awareness had become well-worked and matured such that it percolated through his theology of culture which focused upon the reality of Christian faith. What then is Meland's understanding of the Appreciative Awareness?

Appreciative Awareness

The best presentation of Appreciative Awarenss comes from his book *Higher Education and the Human Spirit* (1953). One particular section entitled "The Appreciative Consciousness" is Meland's formal discussion of it as a mode of thinking or reflecting. One word should be said about the terminology. There is no distinction between the phrase Appreciative Awareness and Appreciative Consciousness. Most often, Appreciative Consciousness stands in tension and opposition to Rational and Moral Consciousness which has been explained from the background of Liberalism. I prefer to use Appreciative Awareness as the attitudinal stance of the person when not referring specifically to its opposition to Moral and Rational Consciousness. I believe that this clarification adds to the understanding of faith as an act of inquiry encountered later.

The concept of Appreciative Awareness is Meland's contextual-relational way of looking at meanings, values, and directives as informed by an aesthetic vision of experience in contrast to the rational and moralistic modes which extricate and distill meaning and value. "Aesthetic" expresses only the mode of reflecting. Meland defines the Appreciative Consciousness as "a regulative principle in thought" which, as an orientation of the mind, "can make for a maximum degree of receptivity to the datum under consider-

14

ation on the principle that what is given may be more than what is perceived, or more than one can think."[4] "Appreciative" conveys the fact that there are no preconceived premises, that categories do not exhaust the meaning of reality or that reality may be reduced to some already defined structure. Being relational in mode, it envisages much that organismic, contextual, or "gestalt" modes of thinking in related disciplines entail. Meland looks for the larger context of reality beyond the person's act of inquiry itself, and a way of being perceptive and receptive to this wider context.

In his chapter Meland distinguishes three types of consciousness which serve as principles of selection or organizing principles of thought in education: the rational, moral, and appreciative consciousness. The rational mode in the Western world originates in Aristotle and is that mode of inquiry which uses the model of intellectual architecture supported by a mathematical conception of universal order. The moral mode in knowledge, religion, and art comes most forcefully from the critical philosophy of Kant. Here is the basis for affirming certain regulative ideas upon which religious and metaphysical ventures proceed which do not reduce to the rational mode. Something of the Aristotelian universal order persists however. The third organizing principle in thought comes with William James and Henri Bergson. This is the Appreciative mode. This principle rejects the premise of a given, static, universal order. It seeks to come to terms both philosophically and religiously with the creative character of the world and its complexity.

James and Bergson act as a dividing line. They are seminal thinkers who assimilated much of the relational mode characteristic of the Appreciative Consciousness. James never managed to completely extricate himself from the Kantian perspective. James' "will to believe" perpetuated the Kantian moral faith. At the same time, James in his *Psychology* uses a different view of conscious experience that Bergson independently formulated philosophically as "duration."[5] As seminal thinkers who break new ground, both of these men awaited a completeness that only later thinkers possessed. One such thinker is Alfred North Whitehead who presents a metaphysical expression of many thinkers who followed the lead of James and Bergson.

Bergson's "Duration"

Bergson's discussion of Time establishes a feeling-tone for the approach to meaning which the appreciative mode implies in James. "Time" is of two kinds: time that is *thought*, and time that is *lived*. Time that is *thought* is easily spatialized for it requires a simple projection from any fixed point of reference, such as sun time, lunar time, or any mathematical construction.[6] Analogously, reality unfolds in like fashion from any fixed point and can be projected by prediction and application of criteria. Bergson uses the labels "mechanism" and "finalism" for philosophies and theologies which use this concept of time. Time that is *lived* cannot be subject to easy projection because too much is involved in the creative moment by which the temporal process moves into the future. The "not yet" of the future depends upon a ripeness and maturation of "what is" coming from the past. The past persists to give character to the emerging event but the emerging event is not reducible to the past. The passage of past to present brings innovation and novelty. Newtonian mechanics accounted for events through causes where time made little difference. All reality would eventually yield to the onslaught of more facts which pieced together the whole. But time as *lived* will not accept this premise. Time makes a difference. Adulthood does not come without childhood, and years alone do not produce adulthood. Something new constantly arises from the matrix of each past moment. The "not yet" remains as real mystery. Bergson formulates this time *lived* as "duration."

William James' Additions

Interestingly, Bergson's writings became known to the English-speaking world through the translation of William James. How much James himself depended on Bergson for the formulation of his own ideas is not clear. But what is clear is that if both are taken together they reveal more than either taken singly.

William James centers on the psychological aspect of the appreciative approach. Two concepts which are formative for his thought and involve the notion of "duration" are: (1) the "stream of thought" with its consequent "feeling of tendency," and (2) the concept of the "fringe of consciousness."

The Stream of Thought

The "stream of thought" has various aspects but "its chief differentiation from earlier theories was its dynamic or activistic character which was, at the same time, given a voluntaristic emphasis."[7] Prior to James, the conscious process had been mechanical in the association of one impression after another. This cognitive theory is usually attributed to Locke and Hume and is sometimes referred to as Associationism.[8] James presented thought as an active and teleological process. The mind is of a piece with biological organism, partaking of its moods and its physiological drives and impulses. Feelings and thoughts are interrelated. As the luminous center of a living organism, the mind is one with the vast dynamic resource of ever-changing meaning. The conscious process has a fluid character that is very complex and difficult to express. James uses the figure of the stream which rushes through time and space like a river in a canyon.[9] But the stream only conveys the fluid character. More needs to be said. At the same time, and this will be very important to Meland, there is a depth:

> There is a constant shading of the luminous stream—now
> everywhere luminous though with a quiet glow, as if the
> whole content of continuous meaning were being borne
> to a conscious level; now darkened everywhere save a
> sharply intensified luminous point as if the full conscious
> intent of the person had become fixed and concentrated
> upon some tiny point of attention.[10]

The conscious span of thought reaches to subliminal depths. "Subliminal" means "under the threshold"[11] and expresses well the interconnection of the stream of consciousness with the organic unity of the mind. Ultimately, James understood this depth to be neurological only: "Like Whitehead, he put the burden of memory upon this sensitized organism, impressing the events of past moments, its tragedies and tears as well as its joys, upon the delicate nerve endings which somehow take up the passage of history into the organism."[12] Thus, the organism bears the precious cargo.

It is important to point out that the Mind for James is not one thing among many in the organism which might be designated "in the brain," but the whole organism seen as a physical body: dormant at times, but at any instant ready to be roused into action as conscious awareness. The Mind is more than an instrument of the moment, however, because it carries the past in its memory which can be triggered and thereby resembles Bergson's "duration." The mind therefore is not simply passive, as in associationism, but active and selective. That which activates the mind in its voluntaristic expression is *interest*. Even the serene, passive moments of contemplative thought have their origins in some form of interest. The stream of thought always has some focus, however distended. Most often it is sharply focused, impelled by some desire or sensory disturbance. It would be true to say, then, that for James, the whole organism comes into play in the act of awareness and gives individuality and character to thought. Thinking is self-assertive in a deeply organic sense that the Stream of Thought tries to convey.

The Fringe of Consciousness

The "doctrine of the Fringe" correlates with the "stream of thought" in James and preserves the fullness of the concept of psychological aspect of the stream. The "fringe" contains the elements not only of the outer range of stimuli which could not come to view in the focused attention, but of the "feeling of tendency" also. The fringe is the threshold of the unconscious, behind which an abundance of accumulative valuations reside as a pent-up resource of attendant meaning which provides a feeling-tone for each

17

new experience. Thus in any span of awareness, the accompanying fringe imposes a vagueness upon thought which cannot be cleared away. This is all-important. Under the rationalistic persuasion, the vagueness is cancelled out in favor of clarity. This holds true even down to practical decisions. James points out that this reach for clarity at the cost of indifference to the subtleties of relations is what has given a false, mechanized conception of the intellect's working. It is what has abstracted Mind from its organic context and thereby created the mind-body dichotomy. The result has been a "too thin" view of reality.

James had understood that what Kant sought in the "transcendental ego" was an organizing principle of consciousness. James claimed that this effort was artificial, dictated by rational concerns because the empirical circumstances were inadequately discerned. By being attentive to the transitive aspect of relations, i.e. to the full content of conscious experience as indicated by the "fringe" with its "stream of consciousness," James arrived at the empirical alternative to the transcendental ego which he called the "feeling of relations."[13] James' Radical Empiricism as it was called asked for a revised concept of the Self based on the view that relations are experiencable. This is the phenomenon of "internal relations" and the *telos* that such relations convey, hinting at an internal structuring of human existence.[14] This is a holistic view where the unity depends upon organic structure, not consciousness, which is a re-evaluation of the importance and interrelatedness of human experience.

Beyond the technical discussion of the mind and self, the doctrine of the fringe opens up the problem of perceptiveness as related to thought, and in opposition to over-reaching precision. As Meland indicates, this matter received little attention, and then only among a few philosophers and psychologists who sought to justify either poetic perception or what was termed mystical awareness which dealt with intuition. As a matter of fact, in Meland's early theological period before 1945, he referred to his own approach as Mystical Naturalism. When poetic or mystical perception emerged, Rationalists emphasized the insecurities, illusions, and hazards of such a methodological appeal by lifting up reason to combat its lack of clarity and murky subjectivism. Neither of these groups wrestled with the issue of perceptiveness sufficiently. In Meland's judgment, James with his emphasis on the fringe along with the stream of thought offers the most impressive justification for sensitive awareness in the cognitional process which is to be found in either philosophical or psychological literature.[15] Bergson labored under the onus of his revived use of "intuition" which expressed penetration of inner meaning for him but never managed to extricate itself from all the additional meanings of subjectivism which eventually resulted in heated disputes. James, with his gift for coining words, managed to present perception in a less arbitrary and controversial way.

18

In James, the many "streams of thought" fit against the backdrop of "pure experience." This position counters the subject-object dichotomy expressed and energized by Kant as the immediate predecessor. James anticipated what the later Process metaphysicians designated as "the social nature of reality," or the "interaction of events."[16] The act of conscious Mind tends to see the self as over against its objects. But for James, things and thoughts are not two different existences but one event seen under different relations to "pure" experience." As James concludes in his analysis of consciousness, "Consciousness connotes a kind of external relation, and does not denote a special stuff or way of being."[17] The Jamesian challenge is not to remove consciousness from the depth of knowing which occurs in an immediate feeling of the inner stream of thought. The conscious quality of our experiences are invoked to explain, and are known by, their relations—these relations themselves being experiences interrelated to one another. In a descriptive passage before James launches into a metaphysical inquiry on the One and the Many, he says,

> The deeper features of reality are found only in perceptual experience. Here alone do we acquaint ourselves with continuity, or the immersion of one thing in another, here along with self, with substance, with qualities, with activity in its various modes, with time, with cause, with change, with novelty, with tendency, and with freedom.[18]

In the discussion of perceptive event which would be used by subsequent philosophers, especially Dewey, James had gone the full distance in his revolt against conceptualism and in establishing his constructive case for perceptive awareness.

Another important concept used by James is his discussion of the "thicker" reality as possessing the dimension of "depth." Depth keeps the inner stream of pure experience, reason, and relations together. James was not satisfied with conscious experience as an attentive act; there is always more depth in immediate awareness than can be brought to the surface. Perceptiveness, then, is not simply a vague portion of conscious thought. Rather, it is more deeply involved orientation of the human psyche in which the report from experience is both full and concrete. To the degree that this psychic relationship is thought to merge with the primordial sensitivity in nature, the report goes beyond mere feeling and opens up profound metaphysical and religious questions concerning the ultimate character of this depth discerned in empirical experience. Meland will capitalize on this insight of depth in conjunction with faith.

James presented a powerful view and vocabulary for the New Realism of the Age of Power. James' tendency toward panpsychism[19] led the naturalists like Dewey and later, Henry Nelson Wieman, to steer away from this same course. Wieman and Dewey moved toward an Instrumentalism of "working ideas" of both God and Value. Wieman, a mentor of Meland at Chicago, uses "appreciative awareness" in his definition of the four-fold event of Creativity.[20] Yet Wieman used tests of observation and reason which yielded empirical confirmation, thereby practicing a reductionism by which the depth of reality yielded to exact findings. Dewey, in his selective Instrumentalism, allowed for feeling but left the analysis as selectively aesthetic. Meland will use these same insights and try to move not in the direction of panpsychism nor in the direction of empiricism alone, but toward a more sensitive grasp of what is empirically conveyed bearing upon an understanding of God within the legacy of Christian faith.

Meland's Appropriation of James and Bergson

Meland sums up the problem, challenging James and Bergson as well as those who follow their lead to lift up the meaning from suffused awareness. For James, the inner grasp, incommunicable and irrelevant to the outer meaning even, was knowledge of a sort though subjective. At least it yielded understanding to the one who possessed it—a feeling orientation which enabled one to act with greater surety and zest than the explicit knowledge might seem to warrant. James investigates the varieties of religious experience from this vantage point. Meland sees James' doctrine of the fringe along with the perceptive ground of thought as a warning against an over-reaching exactness. In James, there is a reaching for disciplined attention such that a measure of precision appropriate to the circumstances of thought is achievable and sensitively sought. Thus the analytic component or critical intelligence must interrelate with perception and awareness. Meland himself agrees and seeks the relation of critical intelligence to awareness such that it becomes unified as Appreciative Awareness.[21]

"Duration" in Bergson is an important concept for Meland. Duration allows one to participate in the depths of realities that are beyond comprehension. One participates at the level and mode of experience which is the meaning of time *lived* or duration. To this extent knowledge comes by acquaintance through bodily feeling and the sheer act of existing, much of which cannot be known in any explicit, rational way. The ultimate range of meaning is not a penumbra of mystery that supervenes upon experience, but a mystery and depth in the immediacies of reality itself. Meland says,

> Attentive moments, alerting and focusing the sensory powers, merely release the floodgates of memory or of judgments held in store through the act of duration,

giving to every immediate event the value and character of meanings that have already accrued. An excess of critical intelligence. . .for example, intelligence dissociated from its bodily feelings. . .will give full weight to each attentive occurrence. Even here, observation is not apt to be a bare event. Something of the substratum of duration persists, or intrudes, even if only as a habit of thought or a limitation of sense to qualify attention and its implications of meaning.[22]

The interplay between duration and critical intelligence is what lifts experience to a creative level, wherein novelty and accumulative meaning become mutually qualifying. This is concern with internal relations which means, "not that one disavows structured meaning to which intelligible inquiry can address itself, but that, to attend to it with any sense of reality, one must employ a mode of inquiry that is appropriate and adequate to deal with structure that is living, that is, dynamic in an organic sense."[23] Whereas Bergson moved to intuition, Meland moved to Appreciative Awareness. The notion of duration was developed as *creativity* in the subsequent philosophies of emergence of Alexander, Morgan, and Smuts. Alexander in 1920 made the first comprehensive attempt to restate the problem of relations in modern terms. Alexander never finished his work. By the time his third volume was to be written, he saw no need for it. Alexander viewed the work of A.N. Whitehead published simultaneously with his to be a fulfillment of his own effort.[24] Thus, as important as Bergson and James are for Meland's thought, additional philosophers and related scientists continually contribute to these insights of the New Realism. One figure that looms large and who contributes to the line of thought from Bergson and James is Alfred North Whitehead. He manages a more complete perspective and lifts his predecessors' insights to a metaphysical system, and contributes to the understanding of the Appreciative Awareness.

A. N. Whitehead

The Appreciative Awareness begins in James and Bergson. Whitehead extends their thought under the new imagery of the Age of Power. Whereas James' imagery comes from introspective psychology, Whitehead's comes from the new physics with its fields of energy. This is a dimension which James generally lacked. Whitehead arrived at his philosophy by way of mathematics and mathematical physics, but it would have been equally possible to arrive at it by way of psychology and physiology, which was the path of James. Victor Lowe lists a number of developments in physics which influenced Whitehead: "the development of *vector* physics, the development of the theories of molecular and submolecular energetic vibration, and thirdly the rise of *field* as a basic concept. Later comes the statistical conception of physical laws, the theory of relativity, and the quantum theory."[25] These elements are all apparent in Whitehead's most significant metaphysical work, *Process and Reality*, in which he extends his thought into a complete cosmology. In his preface to *Process and Reality*, Whitehead acknowledges his indebtedness to Bergson, James, Dewey: One of my preoccupations has been to rescue their type of thought from the charge of anti-intellectualism which, rightly or wrongly, has been associated with it."[26] Whitehead labeled his work "a philosophy of organism." Whitehead believed James could be stated intellectually if one retained the fullness of the context as objective event, as seen for example, in a structure of relations, even as one probed the inner meanings of these relations as feelings. This is quality in structured events which elicit certain depths of feeling because of definable relations. Whitehead insisted upon the interrelatedness of thought and experience even as one focused attention in the act of inquiry. Whitehead's metaphysical rendering of internal relations as "Individual-in-Community" is an attempt to generalize the notion of relations beyond the amorphous stage of James' Radical Empiricism. Whitehead's grades of feeling combined with the recognition of the mutuality of relations between events stated James' notion of "feeling of tendency" and "feeling of continuity." Whitehead's phrases are "prehension" and "causal efficacy."[27] Within Whitehead's perspective, every event, including every person, was envisioned simultaneously in terms of its individuated concretion as a novel event and the communal ground in which the individuation occurred,[28] which has been expressed in the formula "individual-in-community."

Meland insists that Whitehead must be understood in light of James. Whitehead, as indicated, develops and renders James systematic. This insistence by Meland has labeled him more of a "Jamesian" in his philosophical outlook,[29] by critics. More than anything else, the seminal insights of James, Bergson, and Whitehead as the best expressions of the New Realism, provide a philosophical basis from which Meland develops his own theological insights. As a result he is not dependent upon any philosophical basis, but he does extend his theology through their insights which open up new theological perspectives.

Bergson, James, and Whitehead as significant contributors to the New Realism will continually return throughout Meland's theology. Their contributions have founded the Appreciative Awareness in a relational, organismic, contextual, and conscious dependency. What Meland seeks to do is provide a critical methodology for the use of the Appreciative Awareness.

The Problem of Appreciative Awareness

The Jamesian insights of the "stream of thought" and the "fringe" focus on the "More" of experience than can be grasped rationally, thus rendering a philosophical orientation to the Appreciative Awareness. The problem that Meland sees is: "The validity and degree of value which one is to assign to the Appreciative Consciousness that is so weighted on the side of subjective experience."[30] Meland understands that the answer depends upon how seriously one takes the metaphysical truth of the analysis of experience from Radical Empiricism and its successors: namely, that reality is unfinished, that times make a difference, that relations extend every event indefinitely, even making each event inexhaustible in all its relations.

To rescue the Appreciative Consciousness, two sides of life are usually proposed: (1) mechanism and (2) spirit; or the two rhythms of existence (1) fertility and (2) utility; or the two realms of being (1) the world of action and (2) the world of contemplation. All of these manage to drive a wedge between the two sides. For Meland, there is no dichotomy and so a new solution is sought. This is as crucial for Meland's method as it was for James'. Meland says, "The appreciative consciousness as a regulative principle in thought can best be understood as an orientation of the mind which makes for a maximum degree of receptivity to the datum under consideration on the principle that what is given may be more than what is immediately perceived, or more than one can think."[31] In Appreciative Consciousness, there are no preconceived premises that the categories are at hand with which to exhaust the meaning of this object, or that what is being attended may be reduced to some structure already known and defined. Patterns, categories, and criteria are approximate, tentative, subject to revision. That the full meaning of the datum is not given is a metaphysical statement which Meland accepts as one of the components. Yet what is given defies precise formulation and stands inevitably in the context of mystery. "Whether one is speaking of some happening, a person, an institution, the living community, or of God," Meland says, "one is dealing with an inexhaustible event, the fullness of which bursts every definitive category."[32] What then is the procedure of operation of the Appreciative Consciousness in the face of these principles and perceptions of reality?

The Procedure

The starting point for the Appreciative Consciousness is the mystery of what is given in existence. Metaphysically, this could mean the total datum; practically, it means the rich fullness of the concrete event with its relations and possibilities. Meland uses a combination of experience and critical intelligence in tension with one another to probe the cognitive approach of the individual to reality. There are three steps in the Appreciative mode: (1) openness, (2) identification, and (3) discrimination.

(1) the first step: openness.

The starting point of Appreciative Consciousness is the mystery of what is already given in existence. Apart from any already-formulated functional or instrumental use, any rational or moral preference, reality on its own grounds becomes the object of inquiry. It is similar to observing a living organism in its context as it influences an individual. Thus there is an attitudinal receptiveness asked for on the part of the individual toward the datum. It involves the total individual in all capacities—the feeling level as well as the cognitive level. The rational is not the sole factor. What occurs is a type of "presence" of the individual to reality and vice versa. The characteristic of this open presence is "wonder." Another approach is the question: What does this person, this culture, this event have to say? It is a matter of letting the event declare itself.

(2) The second step: identification.

The second step of cognition within the appreciative perspective is the act of identification. Identification means the first awareness of the object comes into relation to the attending consciousness. The consciousness attending the datum receives the communicated meaning within the limited frame or structure of the perceiving mind. Similar to Kant's problem of the mind imposing categories on the "stuff" of experience, what happens is that the datum is funneled into some conscious experience and made part of the internal stream of thought which has been structured already through the process of "symbolization" by which every conscious mind internalizes its objects. This identification step requires a fragmentation of meaning which hopefully will be reassembled by the individual for the fullness of meaning. At the same time, identification implies a sharing to some degree of the feeling-context. It may extend beyond the subjective act of feeling into the event: a penetration of the realm of internal relations where the "me" and the "it" find their common ground in the Creative Passage. Creative Passage will be more important later in Chapter 4. It means the stream of life in its objective dimension. This Creative Passage is the Jamesian notion of "lived experience." This act of feeling into a situation, an event, is an important aspect of cognition. The characteristic of this identification is expressed as "empathy." Meland differentiates sheer thought, sheer bodily sensation, and sensitive awareness. "It is understandable that Kant should have spoken of the categories of mind as being imposed upon experience. In this act of cognition, individuality is both sharpened and asserted."[33] Sensitive awareness, however, is more profound than thought, and more disciplined and directed than sheer sensation. Meland thinks that this feeling context might have been the key that would have unlocked the door which Kant found to be concealing the thing-in-itself. Schleiermacher seemed to be grasping for this key in his emphasis upon feeling as a more subtle approach to relationships with

24

the Infinite.[34] He seemed to be taking account of the deeper dimension of the cognitive process which Kant missed. Shleiermacher, as well as Bergson eventually, slipped in their thinking into the "darkened well of subjective feeling."[35] Meland therefore thinks that James is a safer guide. Meland, in sum, presents a critical tension between sensitive awareness and cognition in the Appreciative Awareness.

(3) the third step: discrimination.

The third step of cognition within the Appreciative awareness is analytical and notes the vivifying contrasts which differentiate the datum into a distinctive event. Even though this step is analytical it does not try to extricate the datum from its context, however, for to do this would be to overreach rational boundaries for the sake of a false certainty or clarity. The assumption which guides the Appreciative Awareness is that an event is never properly known apart from its context. For the relations which make up the datum in its context are as real and necessary parts of its meaning as the internalized core. Both the quantitative and qualitative features of any datum are not only interrelated but also mutually qualifying, If one occurs without the other, falsification in the process of knowing sets in.

Meland is attentive to the fact that dissection and extrication are important components in knowledge. The parts must be reassembled so as to construct the whole again cognitively. The whole is asymptotically understood in its parts. Whatever fragmentation is done, it is done for the sake of the whole. What Meland argues against is the reverse of this order; namely, if extrication from the context is done first, then another type of knowledge occurs. Meland admits that there are different dimensions of knowledge. Analysis of an organism rendered inanimate in the laboratory is markedly different from an analysis of a living organism in its own environment. Although both examinations can be done, a different grade of knowledge occurs in each. The type of examination makes a great deal of difference. Meland concerns himself with the examination of the living organism, in its context, related to life itself. For Meland, it is an oversimplification of the transition between structures that insists on knowledge as derived only from direct scientific method of descriptive analysis. The challenge of Appreciative Awareness is to allow the individual to examine reality, including the individual, on its own grounds as a living event.

These three steps in the use of the Appreciative Awareness elevates perceptiveness to a place of prime importance in the art of thought. It attends to the dynamic character of events and relations in time that is lived. Perceptiveness as Appreciation takes the place of precise calculation in Newtonian physics, where the notions of mechanism and exact principles of inviolable order provided clues to both method and imagery. As Meland says,

Precision, analysis, comprehension, and form are not alien to the appreciative consciousness; but these are but means to an end, not ends in themselves. And as such they are tentative and subject to revision before the great on-going mystery in which our lives are cast—a drama of existence in which wonder, inquiry, and the appreciative mind play the creative roles.[36]

In the New Realism, the dynamic, the unfinished, the incalculable, the immeasurable dimension attending every moment is the most formidable factor to be taken into account. It is the Creative Passage of relationships and events interrelated.

The function of Appreciative Consciousness is both a cure and a prevention. On the positive side as a cure, the Appreciative Consciousness attends every event with a two-fold awareness: (1) with a sense of fact and structure and with a recognition of the descriptive procedure which these elicit; but (2) with an even livelier sense of the intimations of meaning transcending fact and structure to which the measureable order of meaning points, but never wholly contains or exemplifies.[37] In what is an illuminating statement by Meland, the Appreciative Consciousness is made into a special form of intuition or act of faith that sets aside empirical or rational inquiry as being irrelevant to its deeper knowledge. This opens Meland's thought to theological possibilities for the Appreciative Consciousness as a help to faith. At the same time, appreciative penetration of reality cannot be contained in doctrinal procedures and methods. Therefore Appreciative Consciousness has parted company with that mode of inquiry which deals with structures in purely mechanical ways, or that pursues knowledge as if it were simply the tabulated results of descriptive processes which isolate and measure observable data. But it has not parted company with the reality of structure and process. It has rather enlarged the scope of inquiry to pay attention to the dimension of data which each structure and process presents. This, in the end, is a contribution to the discipline of observation and perception. With this approach of the Appreciative Consciousness, there is no need to throw the baby out with the bath water. Meland asks for a re-appropriation of the powers of the individual and the energies of historical development as well.

On the negative side of prevention, Appreciative Consciousness casts out "possessiveness" as a criterion of value. Just as a museum goer can move beyond "I like this!" "I don't like that!", Appreciative Awareness is a skill which can be sharpened through discipline. What is involved is the emptying of one's critical faculties so as to be responsive to what is there. It is analogous to the art critic who grows in sensitivity and artistic judgment through responsible exercising of those skills. The human ego orients and defines the range and receptivity of its attention and feeling.[38] The egoistic person will meet people and situations as so many instruments of his own ends and as extension of his ego. The egoistic parent is the one who sees his child not as a person but as *my* child! Relationships are therefore unilateral and already defined by the individual. The possibility of the individual-in-community does not exist for the possessive person. There is, in short, no way out of the limits of the possessive self. Only empathy and the nurture of sensibilities turn the individual away from self-enclosure. The poison, therefore, of the Appreciative Consciousness is the possessive self.

The Attitudinal Stance

The Appreciative Consciousness is a "disciplined, co-ordinated working of the mind and sensitivities in a way that embraces the relevant and decisive factors in a situation, however, clear or unfocused these factors may be."[39] Meland does recognize the objection that the Appreciative mode connotes an unduly passive character in one's powers of discrimination. In his book *Faith and Culture*, Meland explains his meaning in relation to Dorothy Emmet's "Responsive Awareness" in cultural anthropology. Meland likes the term "responsive awareness" because it is a more active term and "thus expresses better the nature of the religious response to such an encounter."[40] The Appreciative mode is an active mode where feelings and critical intelligence are employed in a mutually informing context. It would be similar to the museum goer who is totally absorbed in the works, finds himself tired, and is incapable of looking at another object of art even though he seems to have done very little for the last several hours except stand in front of pictures. Meland describes the active phase this way:

> Appreciative Awareness means a reaching out toward reality beyond the self and thus is never as passive as the term would seem to imply; but it strongly inclines toward receptiveness to that to which it attends. Yet this act is not passive either—not sheer acquiescence to what is encountered; but a creative act of acquiring unto oneself real meaning of another self or of another object through a process of exercising empathy and identification in a circular movement which returns this feeling-into-another -center-of-existence to one's own self-orientation.[41]

The Responsive or Appreciative Awareness then takes place in a context of depth. It is not so much a cognitive act in the usual sense of a subject attending to an object outside itself but the organism deeply involved in this nexus of interpenetrating relations rising toward a self-conscious identification.[42]

Between Theory and Task: A Summary

This chapter has dealt with Meland's stress upon the change in imagery from Newtonian mechanics to the Age of Power as having tremendous perceptual changes. The Appreciative Awareness developed out of this change in order to answer the needs of the complexity of reality which stands fundamentally in mystery. James, Bergson, and Whitehead represent three philosophers who undertook the task of founding the appreciative mode of inquiry. Most basically, the appreciative mode is an aesthetic mode which serves as a principle of organization in cognitional theory along with Rational and Moral Consciousness. The appreciative mode is contextual and relational and presents a unified understanding of the individual where experience is taken seriously on all levels from feeling to reason. Meland checks the tendency to slip into subjectivism where the individual imposes structure on reality. He does this through a methodological procedure of openness, identification, and discrimination. Recourse to the Appreciative Consciousness is not a mystifying act. It is, on the contrary, "The soundest sort of realism in dealing with family situations, with community crises, or with any problem in society of a complex character."[43] Right decisions usually proceed from some degree of alertness to the moving drama of relational factors: "Usually one says that he played a hunch. Actually, one has attended to the intimations of meaning which appeared 'on the fringe' or loomed as a faint vista when the facts which were known came to be fitted into a pattern of related meanings."[44] Meland himself summarizes his own presentation of the Appreciative Consciousness in a way that will suffice for the last word:

> Finally appreciative consciousness is a disciplined, coordinated working of mind and sensitivities. In parting company with the insistent concern to attend only to clear and distinct ideas, the appreciative consciousness is motivated by a reconception of the realities we experience, and the nature of truth pertaining to these realities. It is the complexity of meaning, arising from the interrelation of facts and forces, which arrest its attention. Attending to the signs and intimations within this complexity one attends to the transitive and relational character. Facts are discerned not in a single entity but in a pattern of relationships which forms the depths of every event of experience and contains resources which point up the tendencies and possibilities in any situation.[45]

In 1945 when Meland took up the task of Constructive Theology at the Divinity School of the University of Chicago, he tried to raise the question of the cultural orientation of every expression of faith.[46] This is the relational and contextual question of the individual toward an overall conception of reality. From his background in Liberalism, Meland says: "The critical problem arising from a reaction against liberal theology has been the repossession of the communal context of faith and inquiry and a reassessment of the relations between the individual experience of faith and the communal witness of the institutionalized faith, the church."[47] What the Appreciative mode has injected into a cognitional theory is a new element to be taken seriously. Faith, as the basis of inquiry, must of necessity reckon with the Appreciative Awareness of reality. If Appreciative Consciousness does not influence faith as an act of inquiry, the faith is an exception to human inquiry. On the other hand, if faith is not more than Appreciative inquiry, then it is humanistic naturalism. The task is set: the Appreciative Awareness is the linch-pin to a contemporary understanding of faith. At the same time, faith is helped and informed by a better appreciation of the human component in its total dimension. What are the boundaries and interrelationships between the Appreciative Awareness of the New Realism and an understanding of Faith as the relationship between the individual and God under that same New Realism? In order to answer that question, we must turn first of all to Meland's concept of Faith.

NOTES

CHAPTER I

[1] This biographical material comes from a letter Meland sent to me in 1978.

[2] The best explanation of the change comes from Daniel Day Williams, "The Theology of Bernard E. Meland," *Criterion* 3 (1964), 3—9.

[3] FFS, p. xiv.

[4] HEHS, p. 63.

[5] Ibid., p. 50.

[6] Ibid.

[7] Ibid., p. 51.

[8] Eisendrath has a masterful explanation of the relation between Hume and James, Eisendrath, *The Unifying Moment*, p. 30 ff. Eisendrath also mentions that James' teleology in thought was one of his contributions to philosophy.

[9] HEHS, p. 51.

[10] Ibid., pp. 51-2.

[11] Webster's Dictionary.

[12] HEHS, p. 52.

[13] Ibid., p. 53.

[14] RF, p. 88; and RF, p. 198.

[15] HEHS, p. 54.

[16] Ibid., p. 54, n. 13.

[17] Ibid., p. 55.

[18] Ibid., pp. 55—6, n. 17.

[19] Ibid.., p. 57, n. 19.

[20] FC, p. 108. There are interrelationships between H.N. Wieman and Bernard Meland which would make for an interesting comparison and some clear differences. Wieman wanted scientific, empirical, objective clarity. Meland thought this theoretical clarity could also falsify the experience. Clarity had to be present on several levels, not simply intellectual.

[21] For all of his criticism against the overreaching of the rational consciousness, Meland does not deny it. As a matter of fact, the balance of the Appreciative and Rational modes is Meland's aim. It is interesting that Meland will not allow for experiential knowledge only, but requires the total person's involvement; hence, Meland's insistence on critical intelligence.

[22] RF, p. 209.

[23] Ibid., p. 118.

[24] Ibid., p. 189, n. 4. Alexander published in 1920; Whitehead, 1929.

[25] Eisendrath, *The Unifying Moment*, p. ix.

[26] HEHS, p. 61.

[27] Cf. Eisendrath, p. 75 ff for "Prehension," and p. 68 ff for "Causal Efficacy."

[28] FFS, p. 43.

[29] David Tracy, *Blessed Rage for Order* (New York: Seabury, 1975), p. 202, n. 102.

[30] HEHS, p. 61.

[31] Ibid., p. 63.

[32] Ibid., p. 64.

[33] Ibid., p. 68.

[34] Ibid., p. 65.

[35] Ibid., p. 68.

[36] Ibid., p. 77.

[37] Ibid., p. 72.

[38] Ibid., p. 76.

[39] Ibid., p. 77.

[40] FC, p. 93.

[41] Ibid.

[42] One of the few incorporations of Meland's Appreciative Awareness into a complete understanding of the person, interconnected with the Rational and Moral components is Donald Gelpi, *Experiencing God* (New York: Paulist Press, 1978).

[43] HEHS, p. 78.

[44] Ibid. Also see C.S. Peirce's abductive reasoning and his similar approach in terms of "musement," *Selected Writings* (New York: Dover, 1966), "A Neglected Argument for the Existence of God."

[45] HEHS, pp. 77—78.

[46] FFS, xv.

[47] Ibid., p. 125.

CHAPTER II

FAITH

In this chapter, I will present Bernard E. Meland's concept of Faith. First of all, it is necessary to present the background of his theological concern. I have chosen to do this through his own assessment of the theological situation in each of his three works which make up his trilogy. At the same time, the three works show a progression in Meland's thought and his attention to different facets of Faith. Secondly, I will present his methodology which he calls Empirical Realism and presents his perspective in theology and its limitations. Thirdly, the definition of faith will be treated as Meland understands it. Finally, since Faith is not a private act simply, but a relation to a reality which has a content in a Church, the content of faith will be opened up for further exploration. The presupposition at work in this chapter is that Appreciative Awareness has raised the question of Faith, but not until a thorough understanding of Faith under the new imagery and new realism has been given can the interrelationship of the Appreciative Consciousness to Faith be examined.

The Context of Meland's Theology

The examination of faith in Bernard E. Meland centers on his trilogy: *Faith and Culture* (1953), *The Realities of Faith* (1962), and *Fallible Forms and Symbols* (1976). Reflecting upon more than thirty years of making, Meland says, "What is insistent throughout all three works is the concern to see religious inquiry as being oriented simultaneously to the cultic and the cultural experiences of a people, rather than being exclusively centered in the cultus of the historic church."[1] The trilogy is a theology of culture: "In a variety of ways I have sought to point up the cultural orientation of every expression of faith."[2] For Meland, this is Constructive Theology which "implies a focusing of theological interest upon immediate demands and concerns of living as these evoke and convey the realities of faith."[3] What then has been the context for his Constructive Theology of Culture?

(1) Volume 1: Faith and Culture

In his first volume, Meland diagnoses a change in Protestant theology. In retrospect, Meland was absolutely right. The eclipse of Neo-Orthodoxy in 1945 took place. The New Realism in theology is a liberal movement not to be confused with historic Liberalism. The new emergent is "the spirit of faith and free inquiry chastened by the fires of war, disillusionment, despair, and tragedy. It has confronted evil that is shocking beyond the power of any reasonable mind to grasp."[4] The concentration camps, the atomic bomb, the devastation of the Second World War converge in an intense statement which has pointed out human weakness entwined with evil. The halcyon years have expired and, in short, a new age has dawned. Out of these harrowing circumstances, Meland sees a decisive theology that must challenge every premise of historic liberalism and declare itself irrevocably at odds with what it calls "a sanguine and superficial gospel."[5] What occurs is a liberal spirit reborn in theological reaction. Meland identifies many of these voices of "reconstructed liberalism," many of whom are members of the Federated Theological Faculty at the University of Chicago: William Pauck, Henry Nelson Wieman, Charles Hartshorne, Daniel Day Williams, Bernard Loomer, and his own writings. This new Christian realism that rises out of the ashes of moral disillusionment and defeat does not leap beyond liberalism, neither is it a sheer negation, nor a reversal. The "Reconstructed Liberalism" is a sober probing of the depths of experience which the more surface-like rational dialectics and pragmatic empiricisms of the Liberal era failed to discern.[6] Faith in this new liberalism is not a rout of reason but a counter claim on the appropriate occasions when the overreaching of the intellect needs to be restrained. "Faith is an initial situation of depth which precedes and underlies the reasoning mind."[7] This critical liberalism sees faith as a primal source which not only nurtures but re-creates, or re-orients, the mind. For Meland, this move toward re-creation of the mind separates him from his own writing before *Faith and Culture*. Before this time, Meland used the notion of creativity, but it was not enough. There is a real energy to faith for the future and a redemptive power. Critical liberalism now speaks out against the lethargy of intellect which ignores basic inquiry that pertains to the life of faith and the elemental, creaturely stance of every individual. What is given in experience must be reckoned with. If complexity in life leaves bafflement, then this hazy element of human existence is a fact. Clarity should not be purchased at any price. To the enlightened mind in the New Realism, Mystery is not an embarrassment nor a stumbling block. Mystery does not preclude the importance of the search for clarity. As Meland states, "In the renascent liberal mood of our time, faith and inquiry become two inseparable rhythms which continually alternate in the course of human experience."[8]

Reconstructed liberalism is Meland's theological project. He then investigates the resources available for the consolidation of the new realism in theology.

(2) Volume 2: The Realities of Faith: The Revolution in Cultural Forms

In his second volume, Meland asks the question whether or not Christianity has run its course. Has the world entered into a post-Christian era? This is a very different question than his first volume asked which spoke for a new critical liberalism and provided clues to its reconstruction. Part of the perspective came from Meland's travel to India and Burma to deliver the Barrows Lectures. The purpose of the lectures which formed the inspiration of the book was a presentation of Western thought concerning Christian faith and its witness to the modern age.

The question of Western culture vis-a-vis other cultures and their heritage of faith brings to light the larger dimension of Christian faith in relation to the energies which sustain any faith. Meland seeks to critically balance cultural objectives and what is sought in the witness of faith. Meland says, "The role of Christian faith is not to decide between differences, but to bring the judgment of an ultimate measure to bear upon all differences motivated by the restrictive vision of self-interest and partisan ambition."[9] Meland maintains that the loss of distance or a sense of judgment has resulted from a conception of the human person formed in response to the scientific outlook dating from the seventeenth century. In other words, the mechanization of nature gave rise to an idealization of the human person such that a responsiveness to saving realities not of the human person's making dissolved.[10]

The corrective is not abandonment of science, but a fuller acceptance of the new vision to which the sciences themselves have come, and a recognition of the powers of its world-view. This new identity has been greatly changed by the new developments in modern physics following upon the discovery of radiation. This has resulted in a new age of power. But there is a time lag between cultural disciplines and scientific contributions. Liberal religious thinkers also suffer from this lag. The result can be obfuscation rather than illumination. The current revolution in cultural forms of thought and experience allow the theologian to illuminate again the realities that are available in the heritage of faith with a new force. Meland identifies and reformulates the vision of Christian faith in this new age. In the new age of power, Meland provides the contours for the investigation of the new perspective.

(3) Volume 3: Fallible Forms and Symbols: Discourse on Method in a Theology of Culture

In his third volume, Meland addresses the problem of the loss of perspective upon the limits of language in technical discourse, specifically related to theology and philosophy. The quest for certainty extends beyond the scope of inquiry. The "dimly focused" should not be shunted or by-passed. Forms and symbols are fallible which have had a purposeful origin. Beliefs, for instance, are expressed in many forms and symbols from myth to pantomime, striving to articulate in language and act what was dimly apprehended. These "playful expressions" gained in intensity of meaning what they lost in range and sensibility.[11] Hence, symbols and forms do not achieve precision and clarity that is definitive. Today, the challenge is whether or not these forms and symbols adequately or even reliably present what inhered in the reality that was experienced, apprehended, or lived.

Meland indicates that, especially in Western thought, "right belief" was everything. For example, the free-churches in Protestantism, and later the liberal wave for whom individual assent supplanted church authority, continued to press for the authentic way of expressing the terms of Christian faith.[12] Among the former, "right belief" continued to be a haunting imperative. For the latter, the appeal to religious experience, to science, to philosophy, or to any discipline became ways of attaining security in belief. In these efforts, the issue of form and symbol emerged though not always in focus or in the foreground. In recent years, they have come to the fore. Meland wants to participate in this new quest through various disciplines where the dimensional and contextual character of knowing and experiencing is seriously acknowledged.

Meland admits that the presuppositions he raises in the third volume actually undergird what was done in the first volume, and in some ways should precede the first volume's thought logically.

As Meland has taken his cues from these descriptions of the problems, his theology responds to them. It is safe to say that his theology concerns the individual, the culture, and the cultus as primary to the understanding of faith. There remains the content of the legacy of Christian faith which needs examination, but not until these other relationships have been presented. From this context of Meland's concerns, Faith may now ask for explanation. But let us first turn to his methodological presuppositions of Empirical Realism.

Empirical Realism

Not until his third volume, *Fallible Forms and Symbols,* does Meland deal with his methodological premises. As he says, "There is a minimal amount of conscious design in what one undertakes initially in one's theological inquiry."[13] Patterns of thought and procedures become clearer and self-conscious in retrospect. Constructive Theology for Meland implies "a focusing of theological interest upon immediate demands and concerns of living as these evoke and convey the realities of faith."[14] The assumption which undergirds this procedure moves us toward the topic of faith: "Faith is to be understood not simply as a legacy of belief inherited from the past, but as a vital response to realities inhering within the immediacies of experiences as a resource of grace and judgment."[15] In other words, faith is alive and well in the dynamics of lived experience today. Meland intends to show this empirically and as part of the new realism which will entail the relationships of cultus, culture, and the individual.

In his early training at the University of Chicago, Meland learned empirical methodology.[16] Meland placed emphasis upon the empirical character of the "mystic experience." "Mystic" here means the non-scientific, nonrational, un-supportable. An example is the experience of worship.[17] As Meland dealt more with relating mystical insight to the empirical approach, he described his method as "empirical realism." At the same time, Meland accepted the empirical approach of William James called "Radical Empiricism." As Meland comments, "To my knowledge, Radical Empiricism was the first metaphysical interpretation of human existence in the West to lift up the simultaneous presence of an ultimate dimension of reality and the humanly imposed immediacies within the stream of experience."[18] The emphasis is on the daily moment of existence which bears witness to an ultimate depth of reality. Influenced by James' approach, Meland tells us of his own development:

> "The basic imagery of my thought, following from this orientation of Radical Empiricism (which I have since come to speak of as Empirical Realism) presents existence in this twofold manner, as embracing simultaneously dimensions of immediacy and ultimacy. On its subjective side, I see existence as a stream of experience; in its objective aspect, as a Creative Passage. I use the term 'Creative Passage' as an ultimate reference in the way traditional metaphysics employed the term 'Being' or 'ground of Being.'"[19]

For Meland, Empirical Realism brings together these various elements such that it can be described as, "a process orientation of inquiry, looking to the lived experience." One immediate difficulty is the meaning of that word "process." Meland explains it thusly: "The word 'process' has never seemed to me adequate to convey what is implied in this orientation; for it singles out the one theme, process, whereas other themes, possibly more important than 'process' are involved, themes such as 'dimensional meaning,' 'contextual relations,' and 'emergent events.'"[20] Empirical Realism always contains this broader perspective of the new realism, and not the technical and restrictive notion of "process" as used by any particular thinker.

Meland came to this understanding through his own development. In the 1930's, he substituted the notion of "Becoming" over against "Being" and thus spoke of his thought as a philosophy of Becoming. Although he still holds this essential contrast in the main, he has come to see that there is no becoming without something that is persisting, giving to every moment of becoming its identity; and that there are periodic plateaus, regressions, and defeat within this stream of experience. Thus he came to speak of "an event of becoming" but it seemed unrealistic. As a way of settling upon a more neutral term, taking account of both being and becoming, thus acknowledging persistence and creative change, "I have come to think of Creative Passage as being the most basic characterization of existence as it applies to all life, to all people, to all cultures."[21] Remember that the Creative Passage is the "objective side" or the empirical side for Meland. "Furthermore, I have come to see the reality of God as being of a piece with the Creative Passage. For reasons which may become clear, I have recoiled from trying to envisage or to define God in any complete, metaphysical or ontological sense, preferring instead to confine attention to such empirical notions as *the creative act of God* and *the redemptive work of God in history.*"[22]

It is very difficult to speak about faith and the reality to which it orients the individual, without making some ontological claims. Meland is aware of this limitation, especially when the method is empirical. In what is an important statement and procedure by Meland as to his ontological claims, he says,

> One may wish to go beyond this empirical line of inquiry to enlarge upon or to give further intelligibility to the claims that are made for it. I have always held that such a metaphysical vision can be justified to the degree that it has some empirical basis: i.e., if its primal perceptions can be said to have a basis in experience or in history. . . On this basis I have ventured to enlarge upon this empirical persuasion by projecting it into a metaphysical vision, albeit a modest one. It is understandable that I should have availed myself of the stimulating imagination of Alfred North Whitehead in this undertaking since he took it upon himself, as he said, to complete the task begun in Radical Empiricism by William James and Henri Bergson."[23]

Many of these elements of Empirical Realism have appeared already in the previous discussion of Meland and they will continue to reappear in the discussion of Faith. The perspective of an empirical approach to faith coupled with the emphasis upon experience under the new realism presents Meland's methodological approach for the discussion of Faith.

The Definition of Faith

The word "faith" has many meanings. One difficulty with the definition of such a multi-faceted word is the reality to which it points, and consequently must be included in its definition. For example, Christian faith has a precise content: the individual's relationship to God. Therefore, there must be the discussion of the content of faith once it has been defined. Prescinding from the content of faith, the perspective from which one defines Christian faith will differ. The Empirical Realism of Bernard E. Meland examines faith within a certain context with the limitations of its methodology. According to Meland's own presuppositions, no one definition grasps the totality of the reality of Faith. Therefore Meland welcomes other perspectives. Nevertheless, his challenge remains to develop faith within the boundaries of his own position.

To begin with, faith overlaps perspectives. For example, faith is used as an attitude, which can mean simply an expression of confidence or an absence of doubt. One has faith in one's spouse, friend, or some enterprise. This is the primordial condition of trust. It can be more empirical: a definite and spontaneous reponse to an accumulative experience with this person or enterprise which leaves no basis of doubt. This is a calculative faith based on probability. Even so, it is not easy to dissociate this "faith" from faith in the theological sense.[24]

Another level of faith, is its use in the cultus, i.e. a church tradition. Faith is the degree of solidarity that may exist with reference to any communal witness. This specifically refers to Christian faith. Meland sees in the earliest records of the witnessing community the use of faith "not so much as a venture of trust against possible odds but as an assurance of grace given in the act of revelation to which the witness is borne."[25] Faith here loses its constant fresh response to a past historical act of revelation and becomes instead a personal acceptance of a communal authority. The tensions in this example lie between the communal and individual attitude of faith, the present and past.

Meland concludes, "In the sense in which Christian theology has most consistently used the term, faith is to be understood as a condition of the human psyche that is bequeathed to it in primordial form in creation and in maturity, following individuation, it is offered as a gift of grace."[26]

Meland presents his own perspective:

Faith, Christian faith, is not a matter of words only, it is energy; social, psychical, redemptive energy within individual human beings, within corporate action among

41

groups, within the culture, expressing this grace and judgment of relationships in terms of the resources that heal and redeem our ways.[27]

From his empirical method, Meland defines faith by both its immanent and transcendent dimensions. On the one hand, to define faith from its immanent aspect means to define faith in a way that relates it "intimately and deeply with the whole evolving structure of experience and its cultural expressions."[28] On the other hand, to define faith from its transcendent aspect means to define faith as a magnetic pull from a transcendent source, an "Other," which alters the course of individual lives and directs them toward a higher order of fulfillment than experience or culture can provide themselves.

Faith as Immanent

Meland defines what he means by Faith as Immanent: "Faith in its immanent aspect is the condition of trust which comes to dominate the psychical experiences of a people, or a person, preparing them to confront the ultimate mystery of experience; or simply to find innumerable instances which awaken man to his limits, his creaturehood, and his dependence."[29] This "condition of trust" is the *primordial sense* of faith given in creation. It is the creative act of God which brings life into existence and imparts the initially subliminal relationships of a life that is in God. This primordial sense is the minimal understanding of faith. Faith in this primordial form emerges as simply a will to live, or a capacity to live, which expresses a joy in living and an organic purposiveness which seeks out conditions essential for the survival of life. The joy of living and the organic purposiveness for continuing life convey the elemental intent of the creature to actualize the relationship with God in an individual life span. This may not even be conscious intent. It is deeply organic and pervades the whole of the living organism. No life is possible without this elemental condition of faith.[30]

Meland has widened the base of faith. It is not simply the faith of the individual. Rather, it is the "psychical experience of a people." Primordial trust therefore manifests itself in other ways; such as, the tradition of a church, or the culture with its art and artifacts, or the human being in communion with others. In short, these "ways" are witnesses to faith, each with an identifiable unity though they overlap. Meland provides the shorthand description of these manifestations as "witnesses of faith." At close inspection, what Meland has done is present the contextual and relational character of a person's faith in its primordial sense given in the creative act of God.

Granting the wider dimension of faith, faith is inextricably individual. The process of becoming a mature human person is referred to as "Individuation." The process is circular: it involves the paradoxical act of falling away from this elemental condition of trust given in creation in order to become a self. "Falling away" is done through self-awareness. For instance, the person distinguishes the "this is ME" from "that is NOT—ME." The individual struggles to become a subject, a self, the intensified self-awareness. The process breaks down or becomes arrested when the person "forgets." In other words, individuation originates from a common web of relationships and cannot cast the self off from them and continues to depend for existence. The movement in the individuation process must include a re-insertion to the communal ground; i.e., the relationships with other persons, other creatures, and the creative ground of being which is in God that allowed the individuation process to take place and in which the person is primordially related. The circle of individuation is complete when the individual grows as a self while retaining its elemental condition of basic relationships.

This condition of trust which is primordial to life can be dissipated. In this case, the circle of individuation is never closed. Such dissipation occurs through "ennui, or the dispelling of it through psychic failure, despair, defeat, or frustration, disrupts the internal functioning and leaves the organism or personality subject to, or at the mercy of, external forces and pressures."[31] Another way of saying this loss of trust is that the person has impaired his capacity to participate in relationships. Meland describes this incapacity as a reversion to self-centeredness. Self-centeredness is the limited ability only to receive from relationships. There is no re-insertion. The individual attempts to live by his own isolation without recognition of the relationships which are there.

The level of primordial trust is faith in its immanent aspect. It deals with the normal human process of self-individuation based on the creative act of God. This thrust is characteristically inward and seeking creaturely depth. The correlative aspect of faith which must be kept in tension is faith in its outward thrust or, better, outward trust.

Faith as Transcendent

The transcendent aspect of faith is a gift of grace which "reclaims man from the alienations of self-experience.[32] Meland's reaction to Liberalism can be detected here as well as his attempt to re-appropriate the historical energies at work. This movement of grace comes from the relationships of the individual to the creative ground and returns the individual back to those relationships in a new way. The contextual and relational aspects so important to Meland's method are at work here. Meland explains, "This is the New Crea-

43

tion of which Christianity speaks, through whom awareness of our life in God is restored, not simply as a primordial condition of trust, though this depth of our creaturehood too is reclaimed, but as a conscious commitment to the creative ground which claims us. Faith in its mature state, then, must be defined as the gift of grace reclaiming us as being related in God."[33] Meland again uses the notion of creation as the source from which faith comes, but this time it is the "New Creation". Or, the parallel exists between the primordial trust which one experiences as a goodness in living and comes from the creation of life, and transcendent trust which one experiences as being grasped by "a goodness not our own" and comes from the New Creation. This is the heart of what Meland calls the "doctrine of creation."

"Transcendent" does not mean a passing beyond history or time, or outside history or time. Transcendence is rooted in the existential experience of the individual involved in the wider, contextual, and related character of reality. This is metaphysically expressed in Whitehead's phrase "Individual-in-community." I think Meland prefers the word "depth" to "transcendence" because depth means involvement in the related nature of reality whereas the word transcendence has meant higher or beyond the order of created, finite, observable reality. Empirically speaking, Meland wrestles with the experience of the individual which comes as a "goodness not our own." This goodness has been identified by Christian tradition as an experience of God. It comes as pure gift, i.e. grace, and value-to-be-accepted, i.e., judgment. Meland will continually refer to this transcendent dimension through these various forms of empirical inquiry.

Faith as Immanent and Transcendent

The bi-polar presentation of faith as immanent and transcendent allows several dimensions to come into starker relief. One is that faith is developmental: from elemental trust in the matrix of life to conscious commitment to a specific goodness in life. To this extent it parallels the Individuation process of the person.[34] Yet the bi-polar nature of faith is not equal because faith as transcendent represents a kind of apex or summit which includes faith as immanent. Basic trust in creation need not include the transcendent dimension of faith. To this extent, the conscious commitment of transcendent faith expresses the whole process of faith most representatively, or better, symbolically expresses the whole process. Meland cautions us, however: "These two dimensions of faith, primoridal trust and the ultimate assurance that comes into the human psyche as a movement of grace are continuous in that they can be considered God."[35]

It is important to notice that although the two dimensions of faith are continuous from the same source, the individuation process precipitates the bifurcation. The developing self intensifies the demands for self-experience and becomes either a possessive self or returns back to the relationships that form its communal ground. This is the circular motion of the individuation process which brings the individual from simply existing to an individual with freedom capable of conscious commitment. Immanent faith follows from creation and allows for the individuation process to begin; transcendent faith follows from the redemptive act of the New Creation and allows the individual to return back to the communal ground in conscious commitment.

A second dimension has been referred to and needs only to be pointed out. Whereas the elemental or primordial level of faith need not be conscious, the matured, transcendent dimension of the New Creation must be conscious. The reason why the transcendent dimension is conscious comes from the fact that the nature of the transcendent level of faith requires a commitment. It involves the cognitional structure of the individual for analytic inquiry along with an act of the will for commitment. Conscious commitment then easily distinguishes the two levels of faith.

Further Dimensions

In its transcendent aspect, faith is a gift of grace which is a dimension of spirit and transcends both experience and culture: "That is to say, it is literally a goodness other than one's own and is consciously acknowledged to be so."[36] Faith then in its transcendent aspect does not arise out of the creativity of existence, or out of culture, or simultaneously with their emergence into actuality. The faith that reclaims individuals issues forth out of the matrix of sensitivity itself that is in the Creative Passage expressing itself through the communal ground, evoking a reconception of experience and culture and of the primordial condition of trust as well.[37] Hence, the primordial condition of trust (immanent) is specified and superseded by the recreative power of faith as transcendent, as it bears upon the entire orientation of the person who continues to grow and individuate the self. Meland expresses it this way,

> Faith, then, we can say is a precondition of thinking
> upon ultimate matters which gives some assurance of get-
> ting beyond the structural limitations of the thinking ego.
> By this one would mean that it provides a responsible
> relation with the ultimate concern on the part of the
> thinker, thereby increasing the probability of his response
> to such meanings or demands for meaning which may
> awaken religious discernment.[38]

Faith then relates the person to the entire datum of reality. Yet this is too general in itself. The Ultimate, in whatever meaning it takes, becomes expressed and committed to in some human structure. The witness of faith is the locus of meaning to life as well. Meland often interchanges "witnesses of faith" and "orbits of meaning." Specifically, both of these terms refer to the individual, the culture, and the cultus. Therefore, reality becomes specified through the individual, the culture, and the cultus such that these witnesses of faith make a significant contribution to the understanding of faith by their presentation of the content of faith. At the same time, these witnesses of faith do not just appear from nowhere. The basis for these witnesses is the "structure of experience."

The Structure of Experience

Meland defines the "structure of experience" as "a static characterization of the persisting valuations of the culture which carry the net result of the cultural history into the present."[39] This "cultural history" means the "continuity of human events that is represented by the generations that move in upon one another."[40] The structure of experience expresses a social fabric which is both (1) progressive transmission of meaning (for example, grandparents teaching parents who teach their children); and (2) a simultaneous interchange of valuations (for example, grandparents learn from their children who are parents and reciprocally parents learn from grandparents such that a mutual interchange beneficial to both takes place). Faith is not something which simply emerges in the human person, it comes from the structure of the human person as given within the parameters of creation. Meland indicates this depth when he says, "Faith is an initial situation of depth which precedes and underlies the reasoning mind."[41] Parenthetically, this use of structure resembles the emergent evolutionist insights of Morgan, Smuts, and Alexander characteristic of the new change in imagery, and the dependence of content upon structure.

Taking a cue from cultural anthropology, Meland notes that faith emerges even before articulated speech. Communicable symbols underlie and precede intellectualized formulations.[42] The social and psychic energies that help structure the person are real energies that must be attended to. Myth is one of the earliest used structures of religious expression to explain the religious experience. Myth then takes on a life of its own and forms other people's structures of experience from generation to generation. Christian faith possesses myth in this positive sense of the word. Scripture is the outstanding example within the Christian tradition. Faith therefore is inextricably cultural. At the same time, culture depends upon faith; i.e., people interpret the meaning of reality through such forms as myth. The accumulative psychical energy of faith in the past that exists through myth is called

46

"Mythos" by Meland. Mythos "addresses a depth of awareness which, while available to conscious experience, functions in the main as a non-cognitive mode of meaning and motivation in the living structure of experience of any people or culture."[43] The cognitive or rational mode of meaning available through an overt inquiry into conscious experience is called "logos." Together they represent different dimensions as well as different modes of meaning conveyed by experience: experience as thought (logos) and experience as lived (mythos).

Granting these aspects of faith which are ultimately grounded in the structure of experience, Meland is not sure whether or not "structure of experience" is a compound term containing faith and tradition, or whether it is more elemental than either of these and stands on its own.[44] "The mythos by its persistent shaping of the complex of feeling, along with other precognitive influences, generates a structured reality within experience in any given cultural history."[45] The structure of experience is the most elemental level of meaning in any culture. The structure of experience mediates the shaping of the mythos and logos as well as the dissonance between them.[46] What is distinctive about the structure of experience is its "livingness, and the efficacy afforded it as a causal factor in conveying this distillation of the lived experience to the immediate moment of creativity."[47] As such, the structure of experience is both selective and inclusive. No event in the past can be completely distilled or assimilated in the present. Even rejection of the structure of experience does not dismiss the efficacy of its energy. For instance, the rejection of divine revelation released into human history is only a conscious act which does not blunt the legacy that persists. Meland says, "The argument toward which these statements intend is that an historical legacy persists with a tenacity and subtlety in shaping the lived experience of a people which renders it indispensable to the culture's identity. However rejected, muted, or ignored, the legacy persists as a mode of efficacy."[48] More specifically, the identity of Western peoples stems from its Judaic-Christian heritage. The problem is to extract the content of the structure of experience.

Meland develops faith from the structure of experience. He insists on the use of history to counter the claims of his own teacher, Henry Nelson Wieman, later a close colleague, who uses "creativity" as a supreme value whereby the future means more than the past or present. Meland emphasizes the present as past attainment of emerging events where qualitative attainment occurs, especially on the level of feeling and interest. In this way, the future is not a preferred value.[49] Emergence is achieved. This is God working in the historical conditioning of the structure of experience, especially in its feeling context of the mythos. The singular affirmation is that faith is the fruition of an age-long venture of dedication and inquiry among any people in response to a persisting concern about their creatural destiny. "More than a set of beliefs, the faith is a set of the mind and an orientation of

47

the human psyche which have emerged within the structure of experience of the Western culture, availing man of resources that are deeper and more enduring than his own creations, for they arise from the creative source of life itself: the work of God in history."[50]

Meland does not want to see faith simply as trust. It is more. Meland says, "Faith, Christian faith, is not a matter of words only; it is energy: social, psychical, redemptive energy within individual human beings, within corporate action among groups, within the culture, expressing this grace and judgment of relationships in terms of the resources that heal and redeem our ways."[51] At the same time, the meaning of Christian faith "is the present affirmation of living Christians, attesting to this formative myth that bears witness to the creative good of existence. It is inclusive of all groups who, in any way, lift up this cultural myth."[52]

Meland has presented a theological anthropology which understands God from the experience of faith. God is the source of creation which forms the basis for immanent faith and the New Creation which is the basis for transcendent faith. A close look will reveal Meland's emphasis on the perception of the human person where he says in one of his favorite expressions "immediacies and ultimates traffic together." But faith in its maturer form of transcendent faith moves from what may not be conscious to a conscious commitment to "a good not our own." The whole spectrum is explored. For the fragile and related nature of faith, he uses the *web:* "Faith as a structure of experience is supported by fragile fibers, numerous tenuous tendrils that rise out of social intercourse like tender shoots. From one point of view this is an exceedingly delicate structure—a web of relations about as tenuous as the spider's finely spun strands."[53] The tenuous fiber is cultural, social, and redemptive—based on something which God has done. Inevitably, nothing escapes its relational grasp. But the problem is clearly to arrive at faith.

Certainly faith depends upon "a goodness not our own." Just as certainly it depends on the individual's sensitivity to respond to the gift. Not only in the beginning is sensitivity required, but also throughout the process sensitivity contributes to depth. Sensitivity must be employed to understand the interrelationships and lift up the primary elements of faith's witness in cultus, culture, and the individual. The ultimate reality of God cannot be cognitively grasped and so the human stance toward the Ultimate must be sensitively approached in some other fashion—namely the total commitment which we call love. The sensitive element characteristic of this perception is the appreciative mode which Meland designates the Appreciative Awareness. Before the relationship of the Appreciative Awareness and Faith can be examined, there still remains the content of faith and its witnesses of faith: the cultus, the culture, and the individual.

Between Concept and Content

How then can the definition of faith be summarized? From the background of Meland's appraisal of the theological situation, faith cannot be examined only in relation to reason. The new imagery has presented a contextual and interrelated understanding of faith in a wider, deeper, and more pervasive sense. Faith most basically is an activity of the individual. For that reason, faith has both an immanent and transcendent dimension. The immanent aspect is based on creation and is a trust in the matrix of life. It may be non-conscious. The process of growth in the individual into a self called Individuation presents faith with another dimension. Faith as transcendent is a conscious commitment to "a goodness not our own" which is not simply cognitive but involving love or religious affections. Faith does not exist in a vacuum but in forms that are historically conditioned, mediated by the structure of experience. As historic, they are also cultural. The energies alive in its historic and cultural matrix are therefore psychic and social. These energies released by the person's expression of the Ultimate contained in myth continue as vital energies called mythos. These are non-cognitive and correspond to Whitehead's feeling-tone called "prehensions" in its general meaning of what carries on into the present. The cognitive energies are contained in the logos. The specific content of the mythos comes from the Christian tradition with its own seminal motifs and metaphors to explain the reality of faith.

Meland is not interested in the initial act of conversion. He remains on the empirical level of having had the experience. Many times faith is mistaken as the experience itself. Faith is not something which the individual possesses. Faith is an orientation of the psyche and even more deeply of the religious affections toward the reality experienced as a "goodness not our own," or a redemptive energy of love which grasps us. Faith cannot escape the use of the act of inquiry. It is not necessarily a lure for certainty which dissolves the mystery of reality, of suffering, or of tragedy. Rather it involves the appreciative, sensitive relationships of the web-like character of reality which will be accepted in a commitment asked for by the content directing and guiding that faith: in our case the revelation of God in Christian tradition. But God is not an historic myth. God is experienced today as that "good not our own." Empirically speaking, Meland describes this depth of reality as the Creative Passage. More will be said about this in the discussion of the content of faith.

Two strong images which deserve mention and will help summarize Meland's view of faith are: (1) faith is symphonic, and (2) faith is an encounter. Meland says that what surfaces when intellectual inquiry and the urgencies of existence are simultaneously in focus is: "The structure of Christian faith is symphonic rather than logical. There is a logic implicit within its minor themes, but the overall movement of its affirmations presents a dissonant situation in which contraries are simultaneously acknowledged and disavowed, in which resolution and peace are somehow attained, but not without the price of conflict, pain and suffering."[54] The symphonic nature of faith helps present the fact that the mystery of God is "disclosed" or pointed at in the sense of Ian Ramsey's "disclosure model."

Faith as an encounter expresses the personal relationships of the individual of faith with the reality of God. No encounter between individuals can ever be cognitiviely summarized. The reality goes deeper than words or thought can grasp. An encounter also discloses the nature of reality experienced in the mystery of God and seeps down to the attitudinal feeling-tones of the individual. Encounter is a qualitative experience dependent upon the capacity of the individual to deepen that relationship. It is appreciative in mode involving the total person: "We live by trust, in part by hope, in part by inquiry, patiently and humbly pursued. And to the degree that these sensibilities of our creaturehood are observed, the pursuit of intelligibility and understanding in the life of faith is a creative adventure full of promise in expanding, sensitizing, illumining, and hopefully fulfilling the pilgrimage of existing."[55]

Faith as a definition remains incomplete. Meland has pointed out that faith is contextual and relational. Faith therefore consists in a legacy of tradition which is centered in a church (cultus), always possessing a cultural witness and dimension, and irremediably related to the individual human person. What then are the "witnesses of faith" entailed in faith?

NOTES

CHAPTER II

[1] FFS, p. xv.

[2] Ibid.

[3] Ibid., p. xiv.

[4] FC, p. v.

[5] Ibid.

[6] Ibid., p. vi.

[7] Ibid.

[8] Ibid., p. vii.

[9] RF, p. iii.

[10] Ibid.

[11] FFS, p. xi.

[12] Ibid. p. xii.

[13] Ibid., p. xv.

[14] Ibid., p. xiv.

[15] Ibid.

[16]Meland was trained in empirical methodology but remained interested in what was called the "mystical" aspect. He called his own early work in the 1930's "mystical naturalism." Bernard Meland, "The Faith of a Mystical Naturalist," *Review of Religion* 1 (1937), 270-78. Meland's struggle with the "mystical" element partially results in his development of the Appreciative Awareness.

[17]Cf. Bernard E. Meland, *Modern Man's Worship* (New York and London: Harper and Brothers, 1934).

[18]Bernard E. Meland, "How Is Culture a Source for Theology," *Criterion* 3 (1964), p. 11. This is an important article by Meland which clarifies several important relationships of Faith to Culture.

[19]Ibid.

[20]FFS, xii.

[21]"How Is Culture. . . ." *Criterion* 3, p. 11.

[22]Ibid.

[23]Ibid., pp. 11-12.

[24]RF, p. 219.

[25]Ibid., p. 220.

[26]Ibid., p. 219.

[27]Ibid., p. 27.

[28]Ibid., p. 215.

[29]Ibid.

[30] Ibid., p. 215.

[31] Ibid.

[32] Ibid., p. 217.

[33] Ibid.

[34] The process of Individuation has been studied in its relation to values and moral training. The work of Erikson, Piaget, and Kohlberg study the developmental aspect. James W. Fowler at Harvard Divinity School has a specifically Christian view, e.g., "Faith Development Theory", based upon these developmentalists.

[35] RF, p. 217.

[36] FC, p. 218.

[37] Ibid.

[38] Ibid., p. 123.

[39] FC, p. 102.

[40] Ibid.

[41] Ibid., p. vi.

[42] Ibid., p. 6; also cf. Peter Berger, *The Sacred Canopy* (New York: Doubleday, 1969), p. 29-31 for his understanding of "legitimation."

[43] FFS, p. 103.

[44] FC, p. 100.

[45] FFS, p. 187.

[46] Ibid.

[47] Ibid., p. 187-8.

[48] Ibid., p. 188.

[49] FC, p. 109.

[50] Ibid., p. 113-4.

[51] FFS, p. 27.

[52] FC, p. 113.

[53] Ibid., p. 198.

[54] FFS, p. 75.

[55] Ibid., p. 24.

THE WITNESSES OF FAITH: INDIVIDUAL, CULTURE, CULTUS

The purpose of this chapter will be to present the understanding of faith in its orbits of relationships beyond its definition. Faith, for Meland, is not simply a legacy of belief inherited from the past, but "a vital response to realities inhering within the immediacies of experience as a resource of grace and judgment."[1] The dynamics of lived experience involve a larger orbit of relationships than can be defined or addressed by the cultus. The form of inquiry for this constructive theology assumes the proportions of a theology of culture. I will present Meland's concepts of the Individual, the Culture, and the Cultus as they pertain to the witness of faith which give an identity to faith and point up the depths of experience which are resources of judgment and renewal.[2] From another point of view, I will present Meland's theory of the human person, culture, and his understanding of the Christian Church which begins his understanding of the content of Christian faith in its historical tradition.

The Foci of Christian Witness

In the culture of the West to which Meland limits his discussion, at least three sources have been formative for the witness of faith. The three foci, or centers, from which response to the themes of the Christian legacy has been conveyed in Western history are: (1) the cultus (church); (2) the individual, often dissonant strands of non-conformity (saints, mystics, and other minority voices); and (3) the culture, itself, notably the cultural arts and music, but even the philosophic lore and sciences as they relate to the primal themes of the legacy, not to speak of industry and the political sphere.[3] These are also called the "orbits of meaning." Meland says, "By orbit of meaning in this context I refer to the cycle of responses giving rise to a complex of symbols and signs, expressed or anticipated, which contribute to a sense of orientation and familiarity in one's mode of existence."[4] There are, to be sure, orbits within orbits according to regions, races, nations and whatever divisions form peculiarities and consensus. Yet what emerge from these inner-orbits are defining limits through historical periods which give rise to culture. The historical sequence of reflection, decision, and action has given rise to a characteristic outlook and style of expression for the cultural experience of the historically conditioned stream of events.[5]

A third description for the witnesses of faith, or orbits of meaning, is a vortex: "the three vortices of Christian witness," or the "three vortices of experience."[6] Although this use of "vortex" emerges in the third and last book by Meland, it has much to offer that the other two words of "witness" and "orbit" do not. Specifically, vortex means a movement that is not only circular (as "orbit" indicates) but also up and down. The importance of depth thereby receives conceptual representation through the use of vortex. Furthermore, the three vortices come from a common source which is designated the Creative Passage in the structure of experience. The stream of lived experience takes precedence.

Meland says the significance of any witness of faith is twofold: (1) it speaks forth out of a primordial ground in which all persons share their humanity, and (2) out of a cultural history that bodies forth not only the commonplaces of its concrete history but the innovations, the peculiar and distinctive intrusions of judgment and grace which its own structured experience has been able to receive and to make articulate.[7] Let us begin then with the first witness of faith.

1. The Individual

Faith does not exist without the human person. By definition, faith requires the individual to be in relationship with the reality to which faith orients the person. Although participation occurs on both the immanent and transcendent level of faith, the transcendent level most significantly involves the person in the redemptive energy of the New Creation and is the summit of what is meant by faith. It is on the transcendent level that freedom is required for the conscious commitment of the individual to the reality of God. Yet the communal and contextual and relational perspectives involve the individual on the primordial level inserted within a wider and deeper dimension. The person thereby exhibits a dual role: the individual as the locus of the faith experience, and the individual as the witness of faith in a relational and contributive role.

The Individual and Internal Relations

Discussion of the human being for Meland partakes of the relationality of contexts. One such context that has been examined before and returns again is the background of Liberalism against which Meland develops his own thought. Under the older imagery of Liberalism, self-experience dominated thought. Relations in this perspective are viewed and determined by their contribution to the individual self. The self, in other words, is the measure of worth. In point of fact, little occasion of real encounter with realities other than self occurred.[8] In the newer imagery of the New Realism, relations are not one-directional so as to exist simply for the self. This is William James' concept of Internal Relations. The theory of internal relations sees every person and thing as related to one another as if all belong in one continuous web. James, and later Whitehead, provided impetus to this way of thinking when they observed that perception contributes a deeper event of knowledge than analysis.[9] Knowledge is not simply rational nor is it totally exhausted by one person, a group, or in one period of history. Reality has a "More" which will not be grasped. Since a total grasp is not possible, reality is complex and mystery is at its basis. Whitehead extended the contextual, relational nature of everything to the ontological statement of Individual-in-Community. Meland echoes these insights when he says, "The mystery of all living is in the realm of internal relations, for these constitute the stream of experience, the psychic flow, the creative flux in which and through which events have their primordial reality. This is the level of creaturehood, a level more profound than consciousness."[10]

The metaphysical grounding of relations expresses the change most outstandingly from relations as external to relations as internal. In other words, relations are not simply chosen by the individual for personal gain. Some relations are given and dictate demands upon the individual. Another way of saying internal relations is to say that relations are experienceable. The individual is simultaneously individual, national citizen, participant in the world's community, creature of creative processes that fashion the whole of existence, and more. One can hardly take each one singly. Together they give the person his complexity. The individual can therefore be seen to live in a depth of relations which compels acknowledgement. Meland himself describes the individual from the view of internal relations this way:

> The minimum metaphysical characterization of man is that he is an event. This means that he is a concretion: an actualization of meaning. Out of the indefinite flow of creativity and innumerable possibilities, he has been individuated as a concrete organism by the gentle hand of a Creator who, in the creative act, has wrested from the chaos and brute force of creativity some measure of order and sensitivity; and from the indefinite range of possibilities, some limited range of possibilities.[11]

The result of these relations will be tension. To some degree, they must be resolved. To some degree, the tensions must be sustained. "I call attention to this point because I believe it is one of the distinctive features of the present view of man. Tensions are real, important, and actually creative of value in existence."[12] Tension is not the end result. It is the condition which holds in focus competing qualitative interests and demands. Such creative tension is the essence of life in relationship.

The individual therefore is totally relational. To understand the individual means to also understand his relationships. Faith itself is relational in that the individual acknowledges a relationship that is truly there as a social, psychic, and redemptive energy for the individual. Individual acceptance of faith thereby mutually influences the totality of relationships expressed by the web concept. The individual, in other words, contributes to the structure of reality and the direction it moves. The individual gives witness to faith as a real relationship not only for the individual but to everyone. Such is the meaning of internal relations when seen from the perspective of faith.

The Individual and the Structure of Experience

The tensions of total relatedness take root in the creation of the human individual. The individual is time-bound and a recipient of the valuations of culture from which personal growth begins which is called Individuation. The individual never escapes the continuous cultural characterization. The word used to describe the structural tensions of these relationships is "the structure of experience." The structure of experience "is a static characterization of the persisting valuations of the culture which carry the net result of the cultural history into the present. The cultural history I am speaking of here is the continuity of human events that is represented by the generations that move in upon another."[13] The structure of experience is deeper than faith and serves as a spatial medium for all that occurs. It points to the re-creative and redemptive resources of living which come from a goodness not our own.[14] The structure of experience exists on various recognizable levels. For example, take the family group. The members talk about the family to others, which is one level. The other level is the one they possess more hiddenly among themselves. Both levels stem from the same set and sequence of experiences that is family history. Family "character" is something else. As Meland indicates, "Character speaks forth out of the spontaneous responses of the person, as well as out of the more durable traits and habits of life. Thus actuality. . . presents history in its stark, creative residue."[15]

It is impossible to comprehend the details of the accumulative valuations of the structure of experience, which gives durable form to our repeated valuations.[16] Thus, the history of events presumes to tell the story of the growth and development in the psychic structure. But compared with the actual evolving structure of experience which is the living nexus of relations in any given moment of time, recorded history is a relatively superficial and impressionistic account.[17] What persists as an organism of events is a selective distillation of what has occurred. The structure of experience is not a blind accumulation of inherited values. Rather, it stimulates an organic unity at every stage of history. Struggles, crises, dedications, betrayals, discoveries, creations, and intellectual triumphs become the formative stuff out of which rise the persisting structure of experience within any community or culture.[18] The present moment is laden with qualitative meaning bearing the living distillation of decisions and the resolution of ages. Each new generation possesses an organic inheritance greater in depth and range than the perceptions of any living person. Thus people live in a context of feeling and awareness that is always beyond their emotional and cognitive grasp. The structure of experience thus can never adequately be described.

Does this mean that persons are automatically bound by this heritage or structure of experience? To some extent, primordial or elemental shaping can be altered, through modification and discipline; but in part it cannot. "To the extent that its shaping goes deeper than man's conscious awareness, it tends to elude the conscious efforts modern men may employ to advance their sophistication, with indifference to elemental demands. And in this I mean to take issue with modernism as such, as we have come to know it in the West."[19]

What Meland focuses upon are the limits of the person expressed through the relational and contextual perspective. Meland summarizes his concern this way:

> Thus any analysis of man's existence at any given time
> conveys but a portion of man's real meaning; for it pre-
> sents only the strands of relationship that can meet us at
> a common level of human response, in perception, and in
> reflection and memory. But our deeper judgment. . .
> leads one to see that this cluster of relationships which
> we apprehend in perception, reflection, and memory, is
> of a piece with the creative passage that carries forward
> all events as a burden and promise of actuality.[20]

The creative passage is a complementary term to the structure of experience. Meland says, "Deeper than the self is the creative passage, the creativity, the on-goingness, the space-time continuum, where the event seems indistinguishable from events. All living is contained in this medium and is sustained as a temporal-spatial event by reason of being continuous with it."[21] More explicit discussion of the creative passage occurs in our later treatment of God. In short, the creative passage is the empirical working of God in the structure of experience.

Meland brings together the various elements of the human person in his description:

> Man is an event in a context of events, arising as a concre-
> tion out of God's creative act. This means that each indi-
> vidual man is a creation, in miniature, carrying the intent
> of God to fruition within the unique pattern of relation-
> ships that make up this subjective span of life. Man is a

temporal-spatial episode in the drama of creation. As such, he derives meaning for his existence from the interplay of himself as event with other events. This interplay is possible because of the psycho-physical attraction and retraction between organisms and the communicative level of meaning that may thus arise out of mutual interaction.[22]

The condition of the creative passage as the context within the vortex of meaning for the individual becomes a decisive factor which discerns the individual's limits: "This sense of otherness as a real, defining, even assertive dimension of man's existence—an 'out there' which may not be altered simply by wishful thinking, or evaded by circumventions of human imagination. The fact of another concourse with the self has become the formidable factor lending depth to self-experience."[23] The individual thus becomes a formidable figure in the drama of events responsive to "a good not our own" in which life is cast, through which life finds nurture, resource, and grace, and by which life is judged.

The concept of the human person thus far relies on the theory of internal relations and the structure of experience. If a sequential presentation could arrange it, the human person participates in the creative passage in the form of the structure of experience which is metaphysically expressed as the theory of internal relations. External relations, though not negative in themselves, would be functional relations that are one-way or unilateral. To continue the sequential process, the individual as a living organism participates in these structural relationships simply by existing and continuing to exist. The person's structure develops through the process of Individuation. The process by which the individual internalizes the meanings and resources of the culture is called "symbolization." "Symbolization" then is "the procedure of creating meaning and of interrelating meanings through communicable symbols."[24] This is cognitive. Creative tensions occur in these processes and relationships which provide the basis for individual creativity in living. This brief sketch of the sequential order if dissected layer by layer reveals that the individual must have a way of apprehending the reality of what has been described. One necessary approach that allows these relationships to exist in integrity is through the Appreciative Awareness. The aesthetic mode of the Appreciative Awareness alone allows the individual the responsiveness to apprehend these relationships.

The Individual and the Imago Dei

The relational and contextual understanding of the self related to the ultimate ground has become   formative   in Protestant theology.[25]

Every person stands related to the Creator, and through this bond also stands related with every other person as creature. In Christian thought, this set of relationships is expressed by the *Imago Dei.*[26] The force of this doctrine that the human person is made "in the image and likeness of God" puts a threefold demand on the individual simply by existing: the person is made for God, for other people, and for oneself. These expectations are given at birth, limit the person as well, and contribute to the individual's complexity. "Birth" takes on several meanings. Meland defines "birth" in three ways.

The first way is the creative intent of God—an expectation laid upon each person by reason of the creative hand which has shaped this emergent, creative event called a person. This is the *Imago Dei* in the form of a sensitive nature, in human structure, to God's creative intent. In the human consciousness, Meland expresses it nicely this way, "This is the cry of the heart, a hungering and thirsting after goodness; and impulse toward love."[27] These sensitive awakenings are qualities of emergent structure which testify in our natures to the image of God at the level of feeling. At this primordial level of immanence by the act of existing, we bear this divine imprint in our natures whether conscious of it or not.[28] Thus we are inescapably made for God.

The second way of defining "birth" is: to be born is to take on instantaneously relations with every other event. The full implication of this "doctrine of prehension is that community is a constituent of the individual."[29] In this sense, we are inescapably made for others.

The third way of defining "birth" is through mystery: birth is not fathomed until the significance of the "I", the subjective self in the context of this social reality, is understood. For there is a sense in which we are made for ourselves. The subjective orientation of the self is a fact more easily graspable. The uniqueness and development of the person is an indispensable doctrine upon which the appropriation of birth in its other definitions depends. Yet the person is limited. This means that the person exists under creatural restictions which characterize every event. The defined limitation of the individual expresses creatural finitude.

To Meland, the lifting up of the creatural stance of the individual with acknowledged limitations is needed. The uniqueness and significance of the individual cannot be emphasized at the expense of creatural relationships. Meland says about this creatural stance,

> By the elemental dimension of existence I mean simply
> living with an awareness of the fact of birth and death,
> confronting man's existence, its range of opportunity for
> human fulfillment, not only within these acknowledged

limits defined by birth and death, but with creaturely feelings appropriate to them.[30]

In order to avoid closing the individual upon oneself, interplay of creatural relations must be exercised. Meland sees the answer in the capacity for *empathy*. Empathy is a psychical capacity which assures feeling response between subjective existences. It means the capacity of the individual to feel into a situation, imaginatively to take situations external to the self into one's private experience in such a way that a kind of transcendence of egoistic barriers is achieved. The individual does this in part by aesthetic appreciation. The Appreciative consciousness in fact begins in empathy, and without this minimum psychical response, the capacity for appreciative awareness could scarcely develop.[31] Deficiency of empathy may result in *schizophrenia* and is Meland's word for a failure of socialization: it is the subjective life turned in upon itself.[32]

The *Imago Dei* as a theological expression of the relationships given at birth, which makes a threefold demand upon every individual, only initiates the theological process. Another theological expression explains the continuing and dynamic relationships of the individual and God. This is the root-metaphor of the Covenant in Chrisitan tradition. More will be said about the Covenant relationship between God and Man later.[33] The point is that in Western society there has emerged a distinctive focus upon the individual. The individual was virtually non-existent in the earliest stages of Near Eastern and Western experience. Personality was corporate and the individual expressed the spirit of a people. Meland says about the Hebraic understanding of the individual, "Personality was a communal term. The individual acquired and conveyed his distinctive, personal identity and expressiveness through the communal experience and history, and was therefore representative of the community. Thus, in speaking of God and man in this context, one was speaking of God and his people."[34] The root-metaphor of Covenant expressed this relationship and is probably basic to our understanding of the notion of relationship which emphasizes encounter as over against mechanical causation. The understanding of the individual away from this communal context stems from more recent periods of Western history such as the Renaissance and the Enlightenment.[35] This concern with personal relationships as an individual corresponds with the passion for freedom.

The Individual and Freedom

Concern for the creatural dimension of the individual points up the limitations given by relationships. The limitations of the individual correlate with the notion of freedom. Meland says, "Freedom is awareness of possibilities and a capacity to respond to them selectively."[36] It is a release from the coercion of limiting conditions imposed by the various parts so as to enable the self to act as a *total self*.[37] Meland regards consciousness as a human structure arranged to make choices. Choice contributes to the qualitative differences that emerge. It is choice that allows the circle of Individuation to close. The individual then acknowledges the relationship to God, society, and even the self. Whatever aids the possibility of choice extends the human capacity of consciousness. This act is creative of spirit.[38] Likewise, whatever crushes, obstructs, or dissipates the possibility of choice lowers the level of consciousness. Therefore, what aids the capacity for freedom, and thus extends the human expression of spirit, can be given in one word: Decision![39] "Decision is the elimination of possibilities and the assertion of one direction of actuality."[40]

The Appreciative Awareness aids the capacity for freedom by allowing relationships to impinge upon the individual. The Appreciative Awareness thereby provides conditions for the emergence of spirit through the decision process. Freedom always entails a release from the limiting circumstances that would otherwise empower what is less than good or of lesser value. The lack of freedom results in mechanism. Freedom allows the capacity for choice: "Freedom is a clear perception of the good and the full commitment to it."[41] Where freedom exists, spirit rises. The conditions creative of spirit are always discerned in relationships. This again is the use of the Appreciative Consciousness but not to the exclusion of Rational and Moral Consciousness. Though the spirit is discerned in relationships, how is the spirit actualized and sustained? For Meland, the movement is always relational and back to the primordial ground of the web-like structure of reality. In one sense, this is Whitehead's Individual-in-Community as the topic of religion which overcomes the fragmentation of life through recourse to the wholeness of it.[42]

Another way of saying the wholeness of the individual is the word relatedness. The primary relation of the individual given in birth is the movement toward community. The spirit is actualized and sustained by a growth toward community. Theolgoically, this is expressed in the command "Love God above all things and *your neighbor as yourself.*" In Holistic thinking in philosophy and psychology, this is the meaning of the human person: "The phenomenon of internal relations and the *telos* that such relations convey, hinting of an internal structuring of man's existence."[43]

In human personality, there are two levels of freedom. The first level is a feature of personality in the human structure; i.e., the process of individuation which releases functions of the individual from the automatic responses of organic life.[44] Imagination, reverie, wonder, and critical thought are the powers of the human person to move beyond functionalism and mechanism. This first level of freedom is the source for much of the creative, national and moral experience of the individual.

Freedom on the second level is the participation of the human personality in the spontaneous and transcending acts of spirit. Here the person is not so much asserting his structure as responding to the "lure of sensitivity that inheres in the relations that form its creative context."[45] As Meland sums up, "Existence then may be said to be possessed of a two-fold freedom, pressing in opposing directions: the one toward possible autonomous self-assertion, the other toward participation in the creative realm of spirit."[46] In this description, the process of individuation becomes the decisive key again as it was with faith.

In the process of individuation, the person freely may not re-insert the self into the communal ground from which everyone comes. The person then becomes egoistic. Egocentricity "is perverse assertiveness of the centered existence disregarding or betraying its communal ground with which initiates the complex of human responses and behaviors which may rightfully be termed *sin*."[47] The person remains unrelieved under judgment except as "a goodness not our own" intervenes as a resource of grace. In this sense, only forgiveness neutralizes the peril of the individual.[48] "Forgiveness as the threshold to the realm of spirit" enables the individual person to receive the grace that is given in relationships. In Christian tradition, the act of forgiveness entails examination of Christology which will be done later. For now, it is enough to indicate that it is the New Creation which Christ proclaims and exemplifies. The good news of forgiveness is an ultimate fact and thus forecasts the person's redemption from the fallen state implicit in individuation. Through participation in the New Creation, the person is reclaimed from the isolationism and fragmentation of human existence attendant upon the individual freedom of each.[49] Meland phrases this well:

> But the redemptive motif not only gives rise to a particular conception of creativity [covenant]; it presupposes a condition in man and in the covenant relation that necessitates a redemptive activity which man by himself cannot provide. An implicit brokenness in the communal ground, following the creative act, and a consequent individuated freedom that both imperils and excites human creaturehood ensue.[50]

Theologically, the "brokenness" or "dissonance" is the theme of the Fall in Christian tradition.

Meland reflects that the perennial topics of inquiry are the same for human beings today as they were for archaic and medieval persons. The realities are expressed through the topics of grace and judgment, sin and forgive-

ties are expressed through the topics of grace and judgment, sin and forgiveness, despair over the magnitude of human evil and the redemptive life.[51] The real development of the individual has not precluded the creatural relationships already given at birth and in which the human person develops.

No individual is completely individuated. No individual is assimilable without remainder to the communal life of culture, nature, or to the activity of God as the Creative Passage. The tendency of every people is to employ the terms of their orbit of meaning universally, i.e., to speak for every one. The limitation of the human response is not only that of creatureliness (finitude) but also of the cultural orbit of meaning which presents the mind within a given area of human association to receive and react to occurrence. Interchanges with alien and rival orbits of meaning occur from time to time; hence, syncretization and secularization are intermittently present.[52] So there is an unfinished character to the individual which cannot over-reach its finitude either in its relations or its meaning attributed to these relations.

Freedom, in many ways, best exemplifies the witness of faith operative in the individual. The individual under this perspective of freedom literally becomes the bearer of grace and redemptive love to others. Conversely, human persons are the bearers of evil, transmitting to one another whatever is expressed through us of the surd of insentivity that resists and defiles the communal growth of love and forgiveness. The matrix of relationships for freedom do not need to be constructed. They need to be discovered. The structure of the human person comes from these relationships, both given and exercised, as in birth and the process of individuation. For Meland, the emphasis rests upon the individual's allowing the limitations of creatureliness to emerge which means to allow reality to influence the individual as it is, on its own grounds. This is the function of the Appreciative Awareness. True, the individual has many relationships that are given at birth. True too is the fact that freedom operates through decisions to overcome sheer mechanism and allow for creative response signaled under the *Imago Dei* that he is made for God, others and himself. Nevertheless, the individual must move toward the appropriation of reality which is an appreciation of the factors at work which provide energy and opportunity for development. The Appreciative Awareness serves this need of the individual and plays a major role in the perspective of the individual as a witness of faith, an orbit of meaning, and a vortex of experience.

Between Individual and Culture

The immanent and transcendent dimension of faith has its locus in the individual because faith is a human act. Nevertheless the primordial depth of existence exceeds the individual structure of life. At birth, the individual finds a whole matrix of relationships that lays upon him the three-fold demand of existence: He is made for God, for others, for himself. The individual gathers up and combines the intent of creation and the process of individuation such that an orbit of meaning emerges. The interplay of human limitations and freedom as a creative participation allows the individual to emerge as a unique person with the capacity to live life in faith. By faith, the redemptive energy of grace and judgment offered and accepted by the individual orients life itself. Though this witness of faith can be distinguished by the identity of the individual, the orbit overlaps other orbits. The communal ground of the individual who is made for others lifts up the cultural dimension when interrelation takes place. This is the second witness of faith.

2. The Culture

The second witness of faith, orbit of meaning, or vortex of experience is Culture. As has been indicated all along but not defined to any extent yet, Culture is an extremely important concept to Meland. So much so that his Constructive Theology has been a Theology of Culture in the sense that he raises the cultural dimension of faith.

Because the individual is basically social, Meland examines the relational and contextual notions of the individual as the first orbit of meaning. In some ways, the individual seems to be primary because faith is an act of the individual. The New Realism acknowledges the interdependence of the primary place of the individual with other relationships given in reality. What "primary" means is only one perspective of the interconnected web. The human person is not primary in the sense that leads to subjectivism, personalism, or where self-experience becomes the measure of reality. This is the view of Liberalism that Meland rejects. The individual is social and therefore more basically interdependent with culture. The creatureliness of the individual is primary as well. Culture allows the human person to develop and receives the development of that same individual. In a very real sense, then, Culture claims an inextricable role along with the Individual for primary consideration. The focus becomes the relations involved which allow faith to occur. What then is this distinct but related witness of faith?

Definition

Meland has remained remarkably consistent in his terminology throughout his writing. His definition of culture has been an example of this. Meland defines culture thus:

Culture is the human flowering of existing structures and facilities, becoming manifest as an ordered way of life in the imaginative activities and creations of a people, their arts and crafts, their architecture, their furniture and furnishings, their costumes and designs, their literature, their public and private ceremonies, both religious and political. It is in their formative ideas, giving direction to their educational efforts and customs, as well as their religious notions and practices, their social graces and manners; in their habits of eating and body care; in their mode of livelihood and the social organization that follows from them.[53]

Meland says that his own definition of culture rests upon anthropological characterizations "which gather up all psychical and mental responses, individual and corporate alike, as being in some sense expressive of the whole spirit of man, susceptible of nurture and culture." This definition emphasizes the role of the human spirit in culture. Creativity at all levels of human concern and effort is monitored, not simply its aesthetic or reflective aspects.[54]

Meland also has a shorthand definition of culture: "Culture, as I use the term, connotes the total complex of human growth that has occurred within any clearly defined orbit of human association, expressing its prevailing sentiments, style, and way of life."[55]

Culture is not synonymous with "civilization." Civilization means a particular stage of any culture. For example, Western civilization has reached a technological stage. Culture exists whether or not the stage of history designated as civilization has been reached. For example, rural areas relatively uninfluenced by technological concerns still belong to and participate in Western culture. Civilization has generally been taken to mean technical adequacy in the processes of society which enables people to live well economically.[56] Though both Culture and Civilization represent particularized fruitions within the realm of experience, Culture expresses the spiritual dimension which is the full range of human flowering expressive at all levels of society.

Another perspective, that of the psyche, expresses another shorthand formula for culture: "Culture, in short, is the corporate, qualitative manifestation of the human psyche expressed through a community at any given level of civilization."[57] In other words, group consciousness in judgments, decisions and creativity come from Culture. The individual is inextricably social and cultural whether in New York City or Appalachia.

The thesis that Meland has come to assert and for which he has argued throughout the years is that "faith is a deeper psychical and realistic event within the culture than this cultic experience, defined and conveyed through church doctrine and history, has made evident, and than theologians generally have recognized. Faith is also more pervasive. . . Much of the contextual spread of its witness throughout culture remains unarticulated and latent, remaining as an overtone of common thought, or an undertow of feeling."[58] Meland rests his method upon the assumption that "our culture cannot extricate itself from the Judaic-Christian mythos."[59] Yet the formulation of a particular doctrine in theology cannot be identified wholly with faith. Faith is more than a cognitive distillation of meaning. Faith is a cultural force. Meland says faith is "a resource of real energy and incentive for the whole of human life which has been shaped in its psychical depths by the valuations arising from its seminal motifs."[60] The "seminal motifs" are the Christian legacy which is the content coming from the cultus, the third orbit of meaning. Meland adds, "What I am insinuating by these oblique remarks is that there are resources within the culture that lend a sense of reality to this gospel of grace and judgment to which the church bears witness, but to which, the church as *church*, and Christians as *Christians*, may be but vaguely attuned."[61]

For Meland, culture is the bearer of the spirit which has been unleashed. Energies unleashed by individuals become cultural too and remain capable of formative influence on others. Culture becomes the matrix. The living energy in culture is the structure of experience. Even the spirit unleashed into culture depends upon the structure of experience in culture. In many ways, spirit depends upon the appreciative modes of human living and refinement carried and given by culture. This is the use of the popular understanding of "Culture" or "Having culture" as an appreciation for fine arts and refinement. As bearer of spirit, culture challenges the individual to an orientation with reality that promotes growth. In many ways, the human person develops because sensitivity and depth occur. The person discovers what it means to be a human person. The most expressive form of this sensitivity and depth is Love. Culture reflects this challenge to the individual and bears the burden of even making the demand upon the individual through forms and symbols. The culture also carries the response of generation to generation within its structure of experience—a deposit of human energies and developments both past and present. Another way of saying this is that culture is a witness to faith both to the individual and to the historical continuity of the unleashed powers of the tradition. As can be seen, the Individual, the Culture, and the Cultus continually overlap and interrelate with one another. Together, they form the witnesses to faith by which a person believes and sustains that belief in relationships.

68

The dynamic passage of events within each culture gives rise to a "structure of experience." It is an enduring structural residue of the cultural history within its particular orbit of meaning. The structure of experience is thus the present immediacy along with the Creative Passage. Meland says that the distinction between the structure of experience and the Creative Passage is comparable to the distinction between "essence" and "existence," though the context here is that of culture rather than an individual person.[62] Diverse cultural currents, each of which with its own dynamic structure, integrated by memory, precedent, custom and its sequence of events constitute a living stream. This process occurs within the Creative Passage. The Creative Passage is the objective dimension; the stream of experience within the individual is the subjective dimension. The primal themes, or motifs of faith, conveyed through the mythos of culture within a structure of experience define and give character to our Western experience as a people.[63] The realities of this faith are cultural forms. It is Meland's contention that Western culture cannot extricate itself from the energies of this faith released as a social, psychical, and redemptive energy. The culture participates in the New Creation under the judgment of grace whether it is known or not. "Religion," Meland says, "generates cultural mythos which works deeply and silently at elemental levels of human sensibility and thought, and thus shapes the culture both wittingly and unwittingly."[64] From the cultural perspective, the content of faith in the cultus has the problem of lifting up and illuminating the interplay of power and goodness in the affairs of men. And within the Christian cultus, Meland sees Christology as the central understanding of power and goodness.[65]

The cultural orbit itself provides the living context in which issues of the spirit erupt and evoke response. Culture plays a role in shaping our encounter with its realities and in giving verbal and symbolic response to such encounters.[66] The symbols as well as the sensibilities of Christian faith have become intimately bound up with the cultural forms to such an extent that to remove the Christian influence or conditioning would be to destroy the form itself.[67] Such would be the case in music, painting, and architecture. Hence, no cultural form or symbols would be spurned as possible bearers of the work of spirit. God's love transcends all cultures, yet it is receptive toward all would be another way of saying pay attention to all sources of the spirit.[68]

Meland holds to a range and reach of sensitivity in the Christian culture of the West wherein God's Creative working is present and exemplified. The pivotal point and summit of the cultural creation of the West is Jesus Christ. Jesus Christ is not an isolated datum as a structure of consciousness. Behind the Christ lies the long history of the Jewish people. Because of this seed bed of moral consciousness, a more sensitive and appreciative consciousness resulted in response to the working of God.[69] In the West, materialism is the problem that challenges this summit of Christ because it ignores the concerns of the spirit and accentuates the practical concerns of a culture out of all proportion to human needs and ultimate good. But the sensitive working of God has been accomplished in the person of Christ. The Christ raises the question of the particular Christian legacy at work in the cultus, the third orbit of meaning.

Culture and Method

The place of culture in Meland's thought should not be underestimated. As Meland says about his own method of Constructive Theology:

> The method of constructive theology has often been characterized as one that begins with an analysis of culture as a way of getting at the primal witness of faith. This characterization. . .does not express the method adequately. At best, the analysis of culture in this procedure can be but one strand of inquiry. Nevertheless, it must be acknowledged that the method of constructive theology pursued within the perspective of empirical realism takes the immediacies of experience seriously as bearing depths of reality expressive simultaneously of an historical stream and of an ontological present, to which response the interpretation must be given. For that reason, what is undertaken in this context is of necessity a theology of culture even as it explores dimensions of the witness of faith which relate to the historical legacy transmitted through the church and to the accumulative thrust of the mythos.[70]

Constructive theology examines culture as one dimension to which theological inquiry concerns itself. In addition, the Individual and the Cultus are part of the strands of inquiry. Meland's emphasis is the cultural orientation of every expression of faith instead of the usual emphasis on the cultic dimension of the historic church.

Meland's substantive use of culture has prompted the question whether or not culture is a source for theology. I believe this is much the same question as the methodological one just raised, but from a slightly different perspective. The answer is interesting and completes what was said earlier. So well-integrated and interrelated is the web both of reality and his theology, that Meland is not sure. The correlation of topics in Meland produces a field theory of its own where many points are held in tension with one another and thereby sustain the entire field. In relativity theory, the point of view chosen becomes the starting point in the examination of the rest of reality in its web-like structure. Culture is the point of view that Meland has chosen. It is inextricable to this thought and theology. The problem for Meland is that the source of theology is the dimension of ultimacy within history and within present immediacies, and that this Ultimate Efficacy of Spirit is received within our structured experience. He can then point up the way in which culture plays a role in shaping our encounter with its realities, and in giving verbal or symbolic response to such encounters.[71] Thus culture seems to play a substantive role for the expression of the Spirit which cannot be separated out. What, in effect, this conclusion signifies is the relational and contextual character of Meland's method. In some ways, it would be fair to say that the interrelationships are such that separating dimensions clearly is never-ending. Thus, in a real manner of speaking, everything is a source for theology where Spirit emerges. This balance of perspectives is a sensitive and perceptive emphasis in all Meland's theologizing. Meland reminds us, "Not everyone will be impelled to relate faith to this wider context of living, or to the deeper and more technical issues of our cultural experience. . . . Faith in its simplest expressions remains a bona fide act with culture, bearing its limitations, but bearing also its own form of beneficence."[72]

The next step, I believe, remains faithful to Meland's position and establishes his particular perspective. Meland realizes the possible cultural accommodation of the idioms of faith and any interpretation faith receives from a theology. Therefore, Meland desires to minimize this danger by insisting on the *systematic* presentation of any topic. The systematic presentation which attends to the total unity of the historical witness thereby avoids many of the distortions and fragmentations that result in accommodation.[73] Meland's method of lifting up the relational and contextual nature of faith lends itself to a systematic theology.

The one step further that warrants attention is that the systematic presentation of relationships depends upon the empirical foundation for the relationships. Though the witness of faith in the Individual, Culture, and Cultus help express the meaning of faith, the ability to appropriate these vortices must be there. Articulation is important but the experience is the key. Only the Appreciative mode allows for the acceptance of reality in the relationships as a mode of experience. What I am stating is that the systematic presentation of topics in the Constructive theology of Bernard Meland depends as well on the Appreciative Consciousness.

3. The Cultus

The third witness of faith, orbit of meaning, or vortex of experience is the Cultus. The Cultus in Western culture is identified with the cultic expression of belief in the Christian Church. The Christian legacy in the cultus is Meland's concern. Meland defines the Cultus as, "The Cult, or the cultus, is generally defined as a particular system of worship, including its body of belief, its organization, as well as its ceremonial."[74] The Cultus provides a unique relationship in the matrix of faith through the witnesses of faith—the Individual and Culture. Although the Individual and Culture are two strands of faith that are mutually dependent upon each other, the Church as the expression of cultus in one form provides the "central vertebrae of faith" for culture and the individual.

The meaning of the church is the organization of a community within the cultural community, bearing and nurturing the revelation of historic events.[75] Meland says about the church:

> The importance of the Christian community within the culture then consists in this, that it bears witness to the message of persuasive love that was released into culture by the events of Christ's life. This Christian community within the cultural community serves to keep the social stream of meaning impregnated with the redemptive force of these events which persists from age to age.[76]

This means that the church is not simply an institutional witness to an inherited faith, or a custodian of a tradition. It is more. It is the actual bearer of seminal meanings which can reawaken people again and again to what is deepest in their nature and in their history by reason of these revelatory events that characterize the Christ.[77] This does not mean that the church is the most effective mediator nor even the sole mediator of these meanings. Sometimes the church formalizes these meanings to such an extent that they are not communicated beyond the cultus. When revelation becomes a possession only for a group, group becomes a sect. Or, the cultus becomes so effective in redefining an orbit of existence for its devotees within the culture that it excludes much that is expressive of human growth in favor of a restrictive orbit. Exclusion, by the orbit of the Cultus, is never totally effective because certain minimal lines of communication between cult and culture are necessary, even if the cultus goes underground. The problem is the perspective that the cultus uses. Independence is impossible by the Cultus just as it is by the Individual and the Culture. The church, as the initial bearer of this continuing revelation, has the responsibility to strive for effective communication to what and to whom it bears witness. When the cultus fails, "such secondary media as literature, art, education, and so on, may seek to replace the church in this role. But these apart from the church can never be as effective in this role as these in collaboration with the church."[78] The vortex of the Cultus has a unique role in the witness of faith but in tension with the Individual and Cultural vortices.

The witness of faith that the orbit of the Cultus subscribes to comes as a response to what God has done in human history. Specifically, it is the experience of the Christ in human history that can never be erased. As an torical event, Meland recognizes the problems of the "historical Jesus" and moves instead to the empirical fact of the experience of those who came in contact with Christ. The experience of the Christ as this new event in human life is what is re-captured in the Scriptures of the Christian witness. This witness testifies to the New Creation unleashed in human history. Such a witness requires attention to the reality on the part of the believer. The mode of attention must be appreciative in part. The Appreciative Awareness attends to the sensitive depths of reality in the Christian witness to the Christ. The Appreciative mode also brings the individual into sensitive relationship with the Cultus and the Culture.

The understanding of the experience of Christ forms the Christian myth, best expressed in Scripture. The church is the bearer of the formative myth as it articulates the importance of the revelatory event.[79] The church's responsiblity is in the degree that it is faithful to this obligation and thereby remains a luminous center of witness within the culture. The church, hence, is an instrument of grace—but a fallible one. The ambiguity of good and evil remains within the church's witness to faith. Still, the church is the body of Christ through which the sensibilities of faith are mediated. In other words, the church is the continuing witness to the revelation of God in Christ as the revelation struggles for communication and receptivity. As such, it is a cultural organism, dependent upon the structure of experience which gives it form and structure.

The witness required to be a church must be self-conscious. Persons can be receptive and thereby participate in the "goodness not our own" without the church. But there can be no church without the self-conscious understanding of its witness which provides an identity. Persons must share this commitment consciously together, or else there is no church. Certainly there are common rituals, history, and beliefs that a church must also subscribe to, but without the understanding that people are one and acknowledge it, there is no church.

Self-consciousness is a razor that we have seen Meland use in other instances. Consciousness divided immanent and transcendent faith, the first and second levels of freedom. The difference between the orbit of Church and the orbit of Culture revolves as well on conscious identity. The difference between church and culture is minimal at times, even indistinguishable when they overlap. Consciousness of the relationship of the individual to church presents one focus of meaning. The church as the body of Christ, unlike culture, *purposely* bodies forth and proclaims witness to the good news that is a redemptive force in life. The transcendent dimension of faith enters here because the individual must consciously accept a commitment to this redemptive "goodness not our own." The commitment is an act in freedom. Identity of those who believe in the historic Christian legacy therefore requires that same conscious commitment: "The Church is a self-conscious

73

community or corporate body attesting to a historical fact of innovation and redemption."[80] In the same way, conscious commitment allows participation in other orbits of meaning. The church, therefore, need not try to separate itself from culture. The culture and church are mutually interdependent.

What is the purpose of the church? Meland understands this focused self-conscious act of dedication as a thrust of spirit and memory within culture which permeates culture with the sensibility and power of the faith. This witness is vocational and purposeful for culture. With this specificity of function, the church is apart from every other social institution.[81] Thus, again, the self-conscious commitment to this witness of the New Creation releases energies of faith into the world. Individuals thereby become sources of grace for one another. Individuals as well participate in a wider range and depth than what is encompassed by church, culture, and the individual.

To convey the contextual character of this New Creaton, Meland sometimes prefers the phrase of Tillich, "Gestalt of grace." Meland explains, "It seizes with vivid awareness that movement of spirit in relations that have been formed out of a common witness to the Christ. It is a holistic instance of New Being wherein the structure of spirit has become luminous in historic events. It is. . . a concrete structure that has become 'transparent,' to use Tillich's term, thus enabling the reality of New Being to 'shine through.'"[82] The phrase "gestalt of grace" helps present the image of grace that depends on a matrix, or gestalt, of relationships. The entire picture of overlapped orbits of meaning, witnesses of faith, or vortices of experience contribute to the meaningfulness of life. Grace operates within this matrix. Grace is not an exception somehow to our experience. The New Creation of God's revelation in human history is persuasive love in Christ as a redemptive energy. The role of the church is unique in its witness to this seminal message of God which touches every dimension of life. At the same time, the witness of faith as Cultus becomes a structured effort. Meland expresses the fallible form that structure then bears. "Religion is the best that we can do in response to the act of faith which bears at once the transparency and the marks of our own ambiguity as creatures. The church will not forsake its expressive and institutional activities in response to the act of faith. But it will pursue these under the judgment of grace."[83]

One important fact that Meland has raised in the creatural dimension of the individuals in the community called Church is that the church understands itself as the community of the forgiven. "Forgiveness may be taken to mean a kind of divine understanding of our plight and our failings by which we are accepted as persons."[84] Forgiveness acts as a release from the sense of alienation and dissociation and enables the re-creative and fulfilling power of the new life of spirit to take over. "This is a power of the Holy Spirit to do abundantly more than we are able to ask or think."[85]

The power of the spirit in the call of faith allows the church as a witnessing community to the New Creation to transcend the barriers of culture. Whereas Meland has confined himself to the Western Culture, the redemptive energy of faith permeating the culture cannot be imprisoned there. The orbit of meaning of Cultus becomes a witness to the world of its ultimate meaning. Meland attributes this dimension to the redemptive love of God, which is part of the revelation, as an energy of grace that recognizes no cultural barrier. In this respect, the grace of God's redemptive love transcends all cultures, yet is receptive toward all.[86] It might also be pointed out that the witness of faith that is contained in culture as the second orbit of meaning must be discerned through the Cultus, or life of the Church.

The distinctive message of the Christian faith is that a New Creation has occurred in human history, releasing into its processes and relationships a new kind of social energy that is both redemptive and fulfilling.[87] The root metaphors of the Christian experience that come through the witness of faith, such as Covenant, Redemption, Forgiveness, Cross and Resurrection, are underlined by love which means the impartial self-giving of God toward his creatures, and the inexhaustible source of grace which this assures.[88] The central point of focus in the historical dynamic of faith is Jesus Christ. He is not just a rallying point for contemporary Christian loyalty and dedication, but a summit point leading back into a drama of history and culture, ultimately illumining the meaning of human life.[89] How Christ was experienced still remains to be broken open.

Summary

The cultus for Meland is the third orbit of meaning. Its place interrelated with the other two orbits is interesting and marks a new difference in the witness of faith. The Cultus comes from the response of the community to an event that took place as an innovation in human history, specified as the revelation of God in Jesus Christ. The other orbits of meaning do not specify the content. The Individual makes the act of faith and, in many respects, seems to be primary in importance. But the Individual does not make a blind act of trust. The strands of faith require the total context of the faith orientation lifted up. This is the gestalt of grace.

No act of faith exists without a content. Or, a witness bears a content which testifies to the one who believes. This witness is not an individual revelation but that which has been borne by the community of believers. This historical event of revelation has cultural structure. At times, the culture has even judged the witnessing community as to its purity of witness. At other times, the culture, in art, education, architecture, music, . . .has taken over the witness to the spirit emerging in the New Creation. The purest form of the witness, however, remains in the community called church. This community forms a self-conscious group whose commitment is to the revelation that God has given which can be re-possessed today. To this extent, it is identifiably different from culture or any of the fallible forms and structures that are used by culture to convey the witness of faith. The church serves as the source of the discernment of the message wherever it appears. The self-conscious community parallels the commitment of faith which is also self-conscious.

Meland understands religion as a very human response to spirit which sustains itself through the growth toward community, hence religion. The challenge of the Cultus is to make the witness of faith as transparent as possible. Hence the church becomes a luminous center where the revelation occurs as a fact. At the same time, the church accepts the fact that the witness is to a "good not our own" and therefore not completely contained by itself. God is bigger than the forms of the church. Faith also becomes a challenge to dimensions wider than the cultus. The acceptance of the limitations of structure means dependence upon the spirit operating wherever it will. The church must therefore be prepared to accept whatever forms culture lifts up as a source and nurture of the deeper life in the spirit. The name is not important. The reality of faith by whatever name is important. Christ still remains the focal point by divine revelatory fact. The importance of Christ will eventually have to be raised in Christian tradition which will put Christ in the correct perspective as the revelation of God.

The community is also the community of forgiven. The limitations of the Cultus are not irremediable. Redemption is a re-creative energy. Forgiveness acknowledges the humble dependence to the "good not our own" which allows the receptivity necessary to the redemptive energy. Left to ourselves, left to our original creation, left to the process of individuation, anxiety, isolation, selfishness, and the dissipation of the spirit result. Only by the working of God in history through the Christ has the New Creation occurred and the Spirit released forever. The form of this event is carried by the Cultus, the mythos of Culture, and the Individual. These witnesses to faith present the content of faith today which can only be appropriated by a person through faith.

Between Witness and Content

Meland's theological method must correlate these three vortices of experience, orbits of meaning, or witnesses of faith.[90] Meland has described each orbit through the distinctive nature of each to contribute to faith. Though they overlap at times, the focus of each can be distinguished. Meland has moved beyond a static conception of faith distilled in the historic witness of a church to a mobile conception of faith dependent upon various structures and the relationships that each demands. Faith then is more contextual and relational in this mobile view characteristic of empirical realism. The creative tensions that result in these relationships more appropriately express the meaning of faith and its dynamic. What has been presupposed is that the ability to accept what Meland has described depends upon our experience which then ratifies the descriptions and insights that have been presented. For Meland, the development of this new perspective of faith depends upon the Appreciative Awareness which allows relationships to remain intact when impinging upon the individual and then be brought to analytical or rational questioning.

One final step in the sensitive relationship of the Cultus must be examined. This is the content of the revelatory event itself that is the sensitive guide toward human life. The meaning of the revelatory event, in other words, expresses the reality to which the act of faith orients the person. At the same time, the content is the relationship of the person to the witnesses of faith—the Cultus, the Culture, and the Individual. The problem of the content of the revelatory event is the problem of God, Jesus Christ, and the Holy Spirit.

NOTES

CHAPTER III

[1] FFS, p. xiv.

[2] Ibid., p. xiv.

[3] Ibid., p. 179.

[4] Ibid., p. 173.

[5] Ibid.

[6] Ibid., p. 157.

[7] RF, p. 348.

[8] Ibid., p. 197.

[9] Internal Relations has a history along with what has been called the "Reformed Subjectivist Principle" in Whitehead which comes from Descartes. The principle says the subject is redefined to include its environment. Cf. Whitehead's *Process and Reality* (N.Y.: Free Press, 1929), p. 179—94, 219—21.

[10] FC, p. 142.

[11] Ibid., p. 132.

[12] RF, p. 200—1.

[13] FC, p. 201.

[14] Ibid., p. 114.

[15] RF, p. 194.

[16] Ibid.

[17] Ibid., p. 194—5.

[18] Ibid., p. 195.

[19] FC, p. vii.

[20] RF, p. 195.

[21] FC, p. 142.

[22] Ibid., p. 135.

[23] RF, p. 196—7.

[24] FC, p. 140.

[25] RF, p. 207.

[26] Ibid.

[27] FC, p. 133.

[28] There is a strong similarity to this "imprint" from another method. cf. Karl Rahner's understanding of the "supernatural existential" *Hearers of the Word* (trans. Michael Richards, New York: Herder and Herder, 1969).

[29] FC, p. 133.

[30] FFS, p. 165.

[31] FC, p. 135.

[32] Ibid., p. 136.

[33] Though Meland does not point it out, there is a worthwhile connection between the mythos and Covenant through what has been seen in America as a "Federal" theology which is the word "foedus" meaning "covenant."

[34] FFS, p. 96.

[35] RF, p. 48.

[36] FC, p. 175.

[37] Ibid.

[38] Ibid., p. 176.

[39] Ibid., p. 177.

[40] Ibid.

[41] Ibid., p. 178.

[42] Ibid., p. 179.

[43] RF, p. 188.

[44] Ibid., p. 237.

[45] Ibid.

[46] Ibid., p. 238.

[47] Ibid., p. 245.

[48] Ibid., p. 246.

[49] Ibid.

[50] FFS, p. 97.

[51] Ibid., p. 81.

[52] Ibid., p. 122.

[53] RF, p. 212; or FFS, p. 155.

[54] RF, p. 308—9.

[55] FFS, p. 155.

[56] RF, p. 214.

[57] Ibid., p. 308.

[58] FFS, p. 86.

[59] Ibid., p. 165.

[60] FC, p. 144.

[61] Ibid., p. 165.

[62] FFS, p. 153.

[63] Ibid., p. 176.

[64] RF, p. 311.

[65] Ibid.. p. 267.

[66] FFS, p. 159.

[67] RF, p. 309.

[68] Ibid., p. 320.

[69] RC, p. 86.

[70] FFS, p. 121.

[71] Ibid., p. 159.

[72] FC, p. 115.

[73] RF, p. 54.

[74] FFS, p. 156.

[75] FC, p. 145.

[76] Ibid.

[77] Ibid.

[78] Ibid., p. 146.

[79] Ibid., p. 219.

[80] RF, p. 314.

[81] Ibid.. p. 318.

[82] Ibid., p. 300—1.

[83] Ibid., p. 305.

[84] Ibid.

[85] Ibid., p. 306.

[86] Ibid., p. 320.

[87] Ibid., p. 267.

[88] Ibid., p. 50.

[89] Ibid., p. 53.

[90] FFS, p. 157.

GOD, JESUS CHRIST, HOLY SPIRIT

In this chapter, I will present Bernard E. Meland's understanding of God, Jesus Christ, and the Holy Spirit. The definition of faith (chapter 2) has found expression in the constructive theology of Meland in the witnesses of faith (chapter 3). There still remains the legacy of faith that issues from the third witness of faith: the Cultus. The legacy of faith needs an explanation of the ultimate reality to which the act of faith orients the person in order to identify the faith as "Christian." Though other elements enter into the Cultus, the most important one is the nature of this God who is encountered. For the Christian, the revelation of God comes from Jesus Christ and involves the Trinitarian relations. In a manner of speaking, God, Jesus Christ, and the Holy Spirit form the most important content of the legacy of faith, that to which the witnesses of faith bear witness, and the orientation of the Individual's faith.

My presentation will be in three parts: God, then Jesus Christ, and then the Holy Spirit. This will not be an exhaustive treatment of the Trinity by any means, but an extension of the legacy of Christian faith as the one to whom our faith orients us. Not only singly but also collectively, there is a need to identify the one to whom reality orients us. And finally, this chapter completes the presentation of faith in its various dimensions.

Part 1: GOD

God and Empirical Realism

In Meland's method of Empirical Realism, "the primacy of experience as lived is emphasized."[1] Theologically speaking, empirical realism penetrates the religious experience to expose the workings of God. God is experienced in the structures of reality as events emerge. In part, the manifestation of divine presence depends upon the human ability to apprehend. At the same time, this divine presence requires identification since it is not any other experience, or the person projecting the self. Identification then requires a response that entails a total commitment by the person to the ultimate efficacy of God. According to the New Realism, "ultimacies and immediacies traffic together" which points up the fact that God's revelation breaks into reality with the limitations and confines of all structured reality. This is not to limit the revelation of God but it does emphasize the empirical presence in its complexity. Meland expressed the most basic characterization of this primal reality of divine presence as the Creative Passage. The emphasis then rests upon God's efficacious presence in the present moment and His working creatively through the energies of mythos and logos in the structure of the past. What occurs is that God "transmutes sheer process into qualitative attainment."[2]

Qualitative Attainment

Qualitative attainment issues from the creative happening wherein past attainment and novel event are somehow made to coalesce, or in some sense to achieve an integration.[3] The valuations and energies of the persisting structure of experience are carried forward into the emerging moment. Meland calls this "character." It occurs in art and religion, in individuals and culture. Metaphysically speaking, Qualitative attainment is "the creative work of God which presses upon every emergent event the possibilities of past attainment; or bends the persisting valuations to the opportunity of creative emergence."[4] The work of God in creative passage is always either enhanced or obstructed by the facilities of the structure and the response which includes both the habits of the individuals and the corporate barriers such as the policies of institutions. God does not work in a vacuum. God works through the available structure of the culture. The cooperation and wisdom of humanity are not in vain but an important part of the emerging process where God is at work. Meland says this another way, "God is on the side of qualitative attainment, pressing its demands upon the impulse toward novelty."[5]

Empirically speaking, God works through the structures of events in which emergence and qualitative attainment must simultaneously take place. God also fulfills qualitative attainment. God is eagerly receptive to the creativeness which presses the past attainment into emerging events, but with a concern that arises out of His responsible relation to the achieved values of existence. The advance into novelty under God's concern brings a continuity with the cultural character and meaningfulness. Therefore it is not enough to examine the emerging event empirically as if quantitatively attained. There is a character, or quality to the emerging event such as a religious experience marked and identified by the presence of God. The movement toward the qualitative attainment is the creative interchange of efficacy called the Creative Passage.

The Creative Passage

The Creative Passage expresses the stream of life in its objective dimension. Meland says, "For reasons which may become clear, I have recoiled from trying to envisage or to define God in any complete metaphysical or ontological sense, preferring instead to confine attention to such empirical notions as 'the creative act of God,' and 'the redemptive work of God in history' . . . Thus I am led empirically to speak of God as the Ultimate Efficacy within relationships."[6] It is most basic to reality. Meland uses it the way "ground of being" or "being " has been used. The Creative Passage is also the most basic characterization of existence as it applies to all life. to all people, to all cultures.[7] The continuous thrust of the Creative Passage can be described as Ultimacy. In this context, Ultimacy is not a nebulous term. "It connotes a continuous threat of the Creative Passage, and is thus simultaneously the present, inclusive of the legacy of the past inherent in its structure of experience, together with what is prescient of its future range. . . Ultimacy can be conceived of under the aegis of 'importance'; i.e., as a dimension of the relational ground of every existent event. . . offering potential fulfillment of its intention. . . or what persists as a concrete destiny."[8] It is within this dimensional character of every actualized event that the mystery of existing inheres.

Meland says about the importance of the Creative Passage: "An underlying thesis of this work is that an efficacy persists within the structure of experience, and within each participant in it, impelling responsiveness to redemptive energies within the Creative Passage."[9] When the Creative Passage is related to faith, the function of faith becomes clear: "The function of faith is to open the creature, elementally as well as critically, to its resources, and thus to avail it of a good not its own inherent in the Creative Passage which cradles and recreates all existent events."[10]

What concerns Meland is an adequate theological presentation under the New Realism. Meland wrestles with the experience of God through an empirical methodology and its limitations. Meland works with the event itself but tries to penetrate the reality through God's own activity in revelation and in metaphysical extension of his thought as to the relationship of reality. Meland opens the possibility for religious experience on science's own grounds without limiting reality to hardened scientific proofs of observation and experimentation. Meland also prepares the individual to accept and respond to religious experience as a wider and deeper dimension of reality. God in the form of the Creative Passage in empirical methodology is the objectifying divine presence.

Meland has come upon the use of the Creative Passage from his concern for creativity. In his earlier writing immediately preceding the trilogy, namely *Seeds of Redemption* (1947) and *The Reawakening of Christian Faith* (1949), Meland developed his theology around the notion of creativity. From such people as Whitehead, Hartshorne, and Wieman, Meland understood and agreed that creativity itself was a highly sensitive and redemptive occurrence. Meland's change came when he moved from creativity, which plays a part, to the redemptive, social, and psychical elements which also recreate and nurture the individual. In other words, there are recreative and redemptive energies that can be re-possessed and unleashed by a life in union with God. The expression of these two aspects theologically is the Creative Passage which explains an ultimate efficacy in relationships. The creative event of the New Creation allows a possession and re-possession of the energies of grace that are social, psychic, and redemptive.[11]

In *Faith and Culture*, Meland has a section that he calls his "credo" of what he believes. In his section on God, he has a summarizing section that is worth quoting to provide his perspective.

> God is a structure of infinite goodness and incalculable power. The empirical evidence of this fact is in the working of grace as a redemptive power which carries implications and consequences of judgment in situations of grief, remorse, suffering, dissolution, tragedy, and defeat; and in the creative experiences wherever a foretaste of fulfillment is attained. The historical witness to this fact of God's goodness and power within the Christian community is the Biblical account of the redemptive work of God in history and the continuing witness of the Church to the good discerned in Christ. The confirmation of this empirical observation and of the historical witness appears when we seek to understand the primordial act of creativity metaphysically wherein sensitivity and what seems to be an ordered concern transmutes brute force into meaningful events. The metaphysical analysis of the creative act of God, implicit in every event of actuality, thus renders intelligible what is given more concretely in the historical witness and in present experience.[12]

God as Transcendent and Immanent

The Creative Passage expresses God's relationship to reality. The experience of God parallels closely the experience of two people in a relationship. The interaction is one of encounter. There is the person, God, and a certain amount of knowledge that is communicated both cognitively and appreciatively. Under the New Realism, reality is not transparent. The complexity of reality described as the "More" by James prepares the individual for the need to discern both contextual factors and human limitations. With respect to religious experience, one difficulty is the problem of the nature of God who communicates Himself in the encounter. One way to say this is God is both hidden and discerned. Another way is God is both immanent and transcendent.

Meland says that as soon as one expresses that God is related to humanity, the immanence and transcendence is somewhat obvious. If not, the result is a goodness without power, or power without goodness ascribable to deity.[13] Or, God is goodness but has no power in relationships; or else God has power but not goodness, acting as an autonomous center of power that disavows relationships. Transcendence and immanence are essential even to a limited and tentative formulation of the character of God, keeping power and goodness together.

God as hidden expresses the movement toward the transcendent aspect of God much the same as an encounter with another person points to a hidden dimension. Meland says,

> What is hidden is the range and depth of the transcendent structure of meaning which is beyond our comprehension. This dimension of God's meaning, our human consciousness and sensibilities with their limited structure can only dimly apprehend. What is discernible is that measure of the concrete nature and working of God which reaches our sensibilities, awareness, and attentive minds. Specifically, it is the concrete working out of creative and redemptive occurrences as these touch our lives in events of joy and sorrow, in experiences of guilt, remorse, judgment, and forgiveness, in the lifting of grief, and in the summit vision of peace, insofar as the human spirit can rise to such fulfillment and meaning.[14]

God as discerned expresses the movement toward the immanent aspect of God much the same as an encounter with another person results in real knowledge and understanding, sometimes referred to as acquaintance. Empirical methodology awaits the revelation of God in whatever form it takes.

The form has been revealed in nature and in Jesus. Metaphysics and Christology are the two routes.[15] According to the new metaphysics with which Whitehead and Hartshorne have been associated, the major problem is one of understanding the meaning of internal relations where the transcendence of the individual event must be seen in the context of its communal ground of being. As might be expected, a concomitant problem is the community of relations transcending the individual experience. In empirical inquiry, a metaphysical vision is justified to the degree that it has some empirical basis; that is, if its primal perceptions can be said to have a basis in experience or in history. Otherwise, what occurs is fabrication, or wishful thinking, or aesthetic taste. From his own perspective of Empirical Realism, Meland projects the metaphysical insights of relations using A.N. Whitehead who took it upon himself to complete the task of Radical Empiricism begun in William James and Henri Bergson. The summation of Whitehead's meta-physics is the concept of Individual-in-Community.

The second route is Christological. This is the aspect of immanence, or God's creative statement within the structure of meaning. Christology illumines God's participation in the concrete events of history, disclosing divine life and participation as immanent in the concrete events expressed as a redemptive and creative power, giving depth and new opportunity to people's lives.[16] Meland presents his own preference within Empirical Realism:

> But if an emphasis must be declared, it is clear that, while the abstract vision of God in his ultimacy is a kind of lodestar holding inquiry and the act of living forward in their courses, the disclosures of this ultimate vision as a fact of experience in the concrete pathos and promise of existence, as these loom in individual and communal instances, form the burden of inquiry.[17]

Christian theology depends upon the strength and character of its Christology. Meland's concern is theology. The correlation of Christology and the new metaphysics is the unique perspective in his constructive theology. For Meland then, constructive theology must include a sensitive and imaginative effort to keep the lines of communication open between the dynamic vortices of the witnesses of faith within the contemporary culture and the witness of Scripture which provides normative content as the revelatory divine communicative event.[18]

Revelation

Christology hinges upon divine revelation. Christology informs the religious experience with a normative statement of how God has taken the initiative in human life. The correlation of divine revelation with the human experience of God produces a qualitative statement of the meaning of God in human living.

Meland explains his understanding of revelation:

> It is my understanding of revelation within the context of emergence, the hiddenness of God refers to the fullness of sensitivity as a transcendent structure of meaning which nevertheless interpenetrates and subsumes every other structure. It is the 'not yet' and 'beyond' of all that is. It is not wholly remote since it is immediate, ever present, and efficacious in every event or occasion.

Yet it is a depth of mystery to which our structure of
consciousness simply cannot attend except in a mood of
awe as in a holy presence.[19]

Meland understands revelation as an encounter "between the
limited human consciousness together with its bodily feelings, and any intima-
tion of a transcendent structure."[20] Moreover, Christ became the mediator
of this transcendent structure of meaning within the human community wherever the witness arose. Christ actually effected the work of God. The human
consciousness, the limitations, the human personality of Christ were the
expressions of God's concrete nature in the world, expressed and transmitted
through human thought and feeling as the revelatory event. Meland summarizes the event this way: "The revelation of God in Christ, then, became
concrete, dynamic, formative, and impelling within the human structure and
in a living community. This was a world event as truly as the atomic bomb,
even though, like the release of atomic power, the facilities for its emergence
first appeared in but one time and place."[21] Almost as a challenge to the
modern believer, Meland observes: "To have Christian faith is to affirm the
reality of this redemptive power as a continuing and ever-present energy of
judgment and grace."[22]

One important basis of Meland's thought emerges. Meland reflects
that the culture of the West has never been the same since the revelatory event
of Christ. A permanent revolution has taken place forever. It continues
today to release people from their restrictive egoism basic to human individuation as well as from the mechanisms of humanly contrived orders of logic and
justice. People can participate in a more sensitive order of meaning despite
the dominating frustration of the human structure.[23] From this vantage
point, Meland opts for the Judeo-Christian myth as more basic to the West
than the Whiteheadean Platonic myth.

Having challenged the Whiteheadean premise, Meland also brings
the heritage of Liberalism under judgment. Meland's concern is the changing
perspective of the basic imagery, in this case, with Newtonian mechanics and
self-sufficiency. Under the new imagery, it is egoism and possessiveness which
arrest the process of meaningful human living. The individual must acknowledge the social reality of relationships which means the self. The individual,
under the new imagery, has a new leverage; one that in some instances deals
better than the old imagery with the facets of reality, and deals with questions that the old imagery could not. Meland cautions that it is not enough
to put into the hands of modern man theological or ontological formulae that
speak to their sophisticated minds. Instead, "it is a matter of challenging this
sophistication of modernity, of breaking through this pose of human self-sufficiency and its facade of intellectualism or aestheticism or scientism which
has enabled modern man for more than three hundred years to stand off from

91

or to appear superior to, the elemental source of man as creature."[24] The response to this concern has been Meland's Appreciative Awareness. The Appreciative Awareness has been a response by Meland which triggers an emphasis upon the elemental, or creaturely, condition of the person toward a relational world which takes experience seriously. In the same way, the Appreciative Awareness enters the theological arena as a new dimension of faith.

Beyond the basic change in imagery which provides a new perspective on revelation, it is true to say that to understand revelation is to understand the experience of those who contacted the revelatory event. This is the community called Church and their expression of that encounter entails myth. Scripture is the best expression of the Christian myth. Christology, as the expression of God's revelation for humanity, comes from the Scriptures. Scripture is not only the experience of the community but also a claim to the faithfulness of what God revealed in the Christ. To have faith is to affirm the reality of this redemptive power as a continuing and ever-present energy of judgment and grace through this myth.[25] Myth, for Meland, is the key to the sensitized awareness on the part of the individual in order to repossess the energies of faith: "It is on the basis of this contemporary respossession of the notion of myth as a legitimate and persistent human response to ultimacy in existence that the modern mind finds its way back to its primal beginnings, and in this return recovers the significance of the Bible as a primal document."[26] The continuity of the Christian legacy rests therefore to a large extent upon the continuing importance and freshness of this myth.

The revelation of God in the Christ finds its most expressive motif in the Suffering Servant of the Scriptural myth. The Suffering Servant expresses the suffering love that God was in Christ and the way that God is toward humanity in the Creative Passage. Meland explains this unifying moment: "The revelation of God in Christ is to be conceived as a perennial experience of the culture. It is a dynamic in the flux of life itself. It is a resurrected life for every age. . . . There is no other way by which this depth of our cultural life can become concrete and manifest save by the recurrent witness of the living Christ."[27]

The symbol of the Suffering Servant most basically states that God is not indifferent toward the world, but participates in the world. For Meland, this is the empirical finding from religious experience from the legacy of Christian faith. Modern Christology, helped by the insights of the New Realism, parts company with thinking about God which makes Him an impassive sovereign or untouchable Absolute devoid of relationships. God as Absolute is a rationalistic bent of human consciousness more akin to post-Enlightenment thought than to other periods of Christianity. The Absolute implies a rational certainty established by logical argument out of concern to find points of fixity and ultimate reference.[28] Under the revolution in imagery,

God's revelation of His involvement with humanity in the Christ can be re-appropriated. As Meland well says, "The essence of God's meaning, and this is the essence of the meaning of Christ as revelation of God, is that God is related to man, that He is concerned, that He is involved in the travail of our critical circumstances. This is not to say that He is involved as we are. . . but He is intimately concerned."[29] Meland has qualified the transcendent "wholly otherness" of God with the immanent revelatory imagery of God's choice that the Christ is the Suffering Servant for humanity who came to seek and to save that which was lost.[30]

God as Love

The central reality of the Christian encounter that issues from the Christological myth is that of Love. The encounter itself is one of sensitive and gentle re-creation extended by God toward humanity. The Christian word for this encountered offer is "Redemption." God is known through the New Creation in the Christ and what is empirically grasped as redemptive energy, characterized by a "good not our own." This is God's love extended toward humanity. On the part of the individual, faith functions to open the creature elementally as well as critically to the resources within the Creative Passage. The conscious commitment by the person in response to God's love is also love. Both the transcendent and immanent aspects of faith move the individual towards love, the latter through creation and the former through the New creation. Yet what form should this love take?

Christ, as the Suffering Servant, identifies how God loves humanity. The Suffering Servant has a claim to symbolic value of ultimate consequence because of its uniquely God-given revelation. The heart of the Christological doctrine can be specified further: it is the problem of power and goodness. Meland says, "The effectiveness of the Christian Gospel in dealing with the problems of faith and culture turns upon the sharpness with which Christology illumines the difficult interplay of power and goodness in the affairs of men."[31] The relational focus of the new metaphysics, for instance, comes under Christological judgment. Suffering love challenges the idolatry of power usually associated with brute force where power is defined in terms of the effect it can cause. The mathematical formula expresses this relationship well: Force equals Mass times Acceleration ($F = M \times A$). It is one-directional, or uni-lateral.[32] Even within the Cultus, dogma and doctrine are not immune from this unilateral power. The kind of power that is appropriate to the life of the spirit is the redemptive energy of faith expressed in Suffering Love. Relations are mutual, or two-directional. Sensitivity and the capacity to receive an effect replaces brute force. Suffering love takes on relationships and the web-like structure of reality as opposed to the isolation of egoism or possessiveness which removes relationships, or better, ignores them. With suffering love, freedom is left intact. The persuasive lure of love invites participation in the life of the spirit as a New Creation of redemptive power present in reality.[33]

Meland understands redemption in terms of the contextual-relational nature of reality from which the individual cannot be extricated, even if the individual chooses to "forget." The experience of redemption as a "goodness not our own" orients the person to respond and issues in faith as a conscious commitment to that "goodness not our own." The workings of God must become identified. The content of the Christian myth informs the act of understanding so as to consciously illumine God working. If there is no Christian content, a nameless "Christianity" of the spirit working still occurs. But the individual related to God with the content of God's revelation brings about a fulfillment in human life: "Human consciousness as a sheer structure results from the refining of physical mechanisms which advance into organisms with a central nervous system; but the miracle of personality is the result of this new emergent; that is, conscious awareness interacting creatively with symbols and signs that designate this concrete abundance of good awaiting human recognition and enjoyment."[34] Redemption, however, is not normal growth. At some point of commitment by the individual, the re-orientation of the person must take place. The person refocuses self-consciousness to a higher center of conscious value.[35] The Suffering Servant expresses the value of God's love through which the person is introduced to the reality of God Himself as the center of that person's life. Yet the question is more than the center of life, it is a question of religious affections: "Redemption as form giving structure to experience in relation to the deepest meaning, which is God, expresses one aspect of the process; perhaps the external aspect. On its internal side, redemption is infusion of feeling. . . . Actually we mean to suggest the subtle emergence of sensibilities in the human being, arising from his religious affections."[36] Most deeply then, redemption is a participation in the love relationships with God which is signaled in the response of the individual called faith. The sensibilities of faith are mediated through the Church which bears the revelatory event of God in Christ especially seen as the Suffering Servant.

Mystery

One final idea that has remained in the background but which pertains to the religious experience of God most integrally in the empirical method is mystery. Empirical Realism deals with the interconnected relationships beginning with human experience. Since empiricism confronts that which the human person apprehends, there is much that our limitations will not allow us to comprehend. Theologically, the individual's approach to God through both the immanent and transcendent aspects of faith respects the fact that their source is one: our life in God.[37] Yet God remains both hidden and discerned as this source. There are limitations in our approach to God even in love. Philosophically, the New Realism of James, Bergson, and Whitehead illumine the relativity, indeterminacy, and complexity of reality. James perhaps expressed this best with his use of the "More" of reality than what individuals perceive. And, although this is certainly an acknowledged area of the unknown, Meland does not use mystery here. Mystery has a more important function than lack of certainty which James and philosophers of science accept. Mystery is reserved for discussion about God. Mystery is not a lack of knowledge, or a type of ignorance. Mystery is more positive. Mystery is the abundance of God. The Mystery of God points up the human limit to the encounter with the reality of God who reveals Himself in concrete reality. Mystery expresses the impenetrable reality of God working in human history which can only be grasped empirically as events where the Creative Passage has become concrete. In another way, human living and loving always participates in and orients the person toward the mystery of God. In a true sense, mystery takes more of an ontological expression of the reality of God involved with humanity than the mere absence of knowledge.[38]

Summary

Meland has remained consistent to his task of Constructive Theology in the examination of the question of God. Constructive Theology raises the cultural dimensions of faith. Meland does this through his method of Empirical Realism. God has both a transcendent and immanent aspect expressed through the two routes of metaphysics and Christology. Metaphysics in the New Realism expresses the internal relations of reality with particular attention to the creative activity of emerging events. Meland calls this objectified creativity of God's presence the Creative Passage. Christology in the New Realism is the historical revelation of who God is for humanity as God in Christ. The Christ event is not a remembrance but a power and energy that continues to be repossessed. The centrality of the message is love which is symbolized in the Suffering Servant. God is interested, involved, and loving toward humanity. The expression of the suffering love of God comes from the Church in its experience which generates the Christian myth of Scriptures. The energy of the power of this revelatory event is extended toward all humanity in the form of mythos. Being grasped by God in His "goodness not our own" is redemption. This encounter begins an orientation of the person to a faith relationship. Redemption requires the faith orientation to move toward love. The individual is then refocused in the higher value of God as the center of life. The sensitive working required of a loving response is also illumined by the Suffering Servant which centers on the interplay of goodness and power in the affairs of humanity. The concern to include relations as mutual and not simply unilateral inserts the person into the social and communal ground of sensitive appreciation of the good that is present in all reality and grounds the elemental stance of humanity. Human life therefore finds the source that nurtures and cradles all life which is God.

In the discussion of God, the ability of the individual to attend to the various factors looms large. Myth, the mutuality of relations, revelation, the Creative Passage, mystery require sensitive attention by the individual to reality. Since reality communicates itself through non-rationalistic terms, the role of the appreciative mode of consciousness is inextricably related to this New Realism. Especially the central message of love in Christianity requires the Appreciative Awareness. For the method of open awareness, discrimination, and identification are part and parcel of this sensitivity required for the love relationship as Christian. Faith, the Appreciative Awareness, and the content of faith contribute to the response of the individual to the reality of God.

Between God and Christ

Under the New Realism, the theory of relativity states that reality can be seen from many different perspectives. In Meland's theology, both the perspective and the relations that it has are attended to. The choice of one topic will lead to interconnected other topics. Together, they form his systematic theology which helps provide the balance that avoids distortion as much as possible. In this relational-contextual theology, many of the same topics return from many different perspectives. The question of God, for instance, involves the question of the Christ. This is from the chosen perspective of God. It is legitimate to choose the perspective of the Christ which will involve the question of God. I think that this is an important dimension and insight of Meland's theological method, and hence his theology. I have tried to remain faithful to it throughout my own presentation of Meland. I think that this relational nature of theology is perhaps best exemplified in these two sections on God and the Christ.

Part 2: Jesus Christ

No understanding of Christian theology is complete without an examination and explanation of Jesus Christ. For, after all, it is the Christ event that gives force and character to the faith of those who are called "Christians." Meland expresses this position as "the strength of one's theology turns upon Christology." Christology expresses the summit of revelation. On the one hand, Christology enlightens humanity's relation to God by revealing who God is toward humanity. On the other hand, the event of God in history came irrevocably in Jesus. The experience of the Christ becomes the focal point of faith. The legacy of faith that has been sustained is tradition. The tradition, or legacy of faith, in its forms of Scriptural myth and the energies of the myth which persist as mythos challenge the meaning of life and bring it under judgment. Through Christology under its various witnesses of the tradition (Cultus), culture, and the individual believer, a specific identity of the reality to which faith orients the person emerges to which the individual, culture, and cultus must remain faithful witnesses.

The Christ-event may not be the starting point for every Christian, or for every theologian: "That which prompts one to be theologically reflective or inquiring may be a specific occurrence in one's experience, some situation of impasse or crisis, of release or heightening."[39] The living context comes from the cultural scene. Whether it is a conflict of judgment over human rights, inhuman circumstances or acts which threaten the integrity of human relationships, the Spirit erupts and evokes response. The summit of this cultural creation in Western culture is Jesus Christ who is also the pivotal point.[40] As the summit, Christ is the focal point forever of the Christian myth. And as the pivotal point, Christ is the source of faith. Another way of saying this is that Christ is the luminous point in our culture that attests to the good that may be more widely discerned, and even first discerned in empirical experience.[41] In this instance, Christ is normative for all experience of faith even if he remains nameless. The energy of Christian faith mounts in proportion to the sustaining, concrete good in existence which becomes real to us. Theories of God, doctrines of faith, even Christologies miss the point "until the concrete fullness of this pervasive good in existence reaches us as an empirical reality with which we can live, upon which we can rely, and to which we can have recourse, not only in days of disaster but in every day that we live." Christ, then, is not a mere idea, imagination, or theological concept. This would be to stunt the whole other dimension of Christ as a real energy released into history forever which can be repossessed. Christ is event, fact, actuality. Meland likes Whitehead's description of the event of Christ: Christ is "an eruption in history in which the good that is in God and the tendernesses of mere life itself came visibly to view."[42] Yet Christ did not disavow the reality of all existence, as a miracle, but entered into life abundantly lived and death tragically embraced. "This was real man, real human existence reaching its magnitude in achieving access to the concrete abundance of good."[43]

Christ then becomes revelation but in two dimensions, not one. First of all, Christ reveals God and secondly Christ reveals man. Christ brings to the fore in one concrete span of life the intent of creation where the tender working of God is actualized in a human structure of consciousness and made creative of a community of love.[44] Christ becomes the summit of God's coming to humanity and humanity reaching toward God. As such, Christ holds the unique position forever as the nexus.

Christ as the source of faith for the individual returns the individual to the concrete depths of his own existence. Meland explains this movement through the image of the "aperture": "By his love we are redeemed in the sense that this aperture, this tiny point of existential witness to God's working in ourselves is given fullness of meaning and we, as subjective selves, are overcome with goodness in the same way that brute force, in the act of creation, yields to God's working, thus issuing in creative events."[45] The movement is outward from the individual which is the elemental stance of the human person in a relational reality. The meaning of life draws upon and depends upon the relational character of reality expressed through depth. The form-giving process is the redemptive process and it works just the same way that creation changes the formless into structures of meaning. The principle of the new Christocentric organization in the New Creation is love, especially the suffering love of God expressed in the Christ.

Although it may seem overly obvious, God was not rendered more sensitive as saving love or as Suffering Servant by Jesus Christ; He was disclosed as such. This means to Meland that what became actual and historical in Jesus Christ as an expression of who God is toward humanity had ontological reality prior to the emergence of structures adequate for its disclosure within history.[46] God was suffering love even before humanity understood.

Meland admits that God's prior nature of suffering love is not strictly empirical. It rests upon the extension of the philosophy of organism in its metaphysical aspects. Specifically, the historical event is of a piece with what is given as an ontological description of God as the primordial ground of existence. Or, as Meland says from the theological perspective about the ontological structure: "The sensitivity of relations expressed as the energy of grace and of saving love in Jesus Christ as Suffering Servant is a dimension of being, spirit, freedom, or creativity supervening or undergirding existence itself. Created beings like ourselves exist by reason of this matrix of sensibility."[47] In other words, the revelation of Christ was not an exception but an expression of what is most basic to humanity. The web-like character of all reality which takes relations seriously and the Individual-in-Community as ontologically expressive, views God as the basis of existence. Revelation in Christ has disclosed the way God is related to humanity. God's already existing relation to humanity becomes expressed in Jesus Christ and in turn becomes an energy of New Creation in the lives of people.

In Meland's theology, the doctrine of creation plays an important part. The doctrine of creation formed the basis for his two dimensions of faith as immanent and transcendent. The use of the word "New Creation" in Meland is the revelatory event of the Christ which can be repossessed as a redemptive energy in individuals' lives. Meland prefers the term "New Creation" because it is biblical and rooted in the Christian myth as an expression of the newness about our relation with God.[48] Meland does not ignore the sequence of happenings with Judaic history that allowed this radical innovation of Christ within the structure of experience to become possible.[49] The New Creation is the redemptive theme defining and forming the Judaic-Christian perspective upon the experience of human life. The events of the Hebraic-Christian history are the empirical roots of this redemptive motif. In another view, God's efficacy has been recorded in interaction with history. The climactic theme of the Christian rendering of the drama of redemption is the Easter myth of the resurrection: "Its structural meaning is an affirming note beyond tragedy, a living forward in trust, despite the immediacies of anguish and defeat. It is a final declaration of hope in the relational ground of the covenant, namely, that our life is in God, and, to the Jew as well as to the Christian, it has given a sense of openness and expectancy transcending the closures and despairs of experience and history."[50]

The sensitive and tender expression of God in Christ as suffering love has its counterpart in the new metaphysical thinkers such as Whitehead, Hartshorne, and Wieman. For, without a Christology, one must turn to a theory of value, or an empirical criterion of God's working in history, or some other normative measure by which a selective view of good and evil, grace and judgment in existence can be established. In Christology, however, God is not in terms of logical perfection but God in His concreteness, reconciling the world to Himself, taking the form and burden of becoming human. Through Christology, the Christian gospel comes to terms with the fact that we are born into a world of insensitivity, terror, and cruelty. In short, we are born into a situation of sickness and health, of growth and decay, of hope and despair.[51] The starting point to interpret the themes of the Christian faith constructively returns: one will move between an ontological vision of God in his ultimacy and a Christological vision of God in his immediacy.[52]

Two themes in Christology need reiteration from the Christological perspective. The first is Forgiveness. The function of forgiveness is the empirical threshold of the realm of spirit operating in this matrix of sensitivity for good. Christology enters into human history and allows the reality of spirit to transform the individual into a new creation. Christology cuts inroads at this point. For it is the New Creation in Christ that proclaims and exemplifies the good news of forgiveness as an ultimate fact, and thus foretells humanity's redemption from the fallen state implicit in every act of individuation. Through participation in the New Creation, the person is reclaimed from the isolationism and fragmentation of human existence. Pain, tragedy, suffering, and limitations are not removed. The individual's own freedom is actualized to become attendant to a higher level of freedom in relationships.[53] The demands of "birth" according to the metaphysics of Internal Relations, which understands the person relationally, and the notion of Covenant in terms of its derivative, the *Imago Dei*, place the three-fold burden upon every individual: he is made for God, for others, for himself. The theological notion of the Fall indicates the need for healing and mending which is expressed as forgiveness.

The process of individuation is the source of our Fallenness, or — "what" is forgiven. "Who" forgives is equally important. Christology explains the suffering love of God extended to humanity as the one who forgives because He is the one who loves. Forgiveness by God moves us toward love. The love that is required expresses itself in the three-fold demand of love of God, love of others, and love of self. The individual moves away from "possessiveness" or "egoism" to the inescapable relationships that must be accepted. Christology exemplifies the quality of response in love to those relationships with God, others, and the self. Indeed, the revelation of God is a message integral for life. The experience of forgiveness is part of that message.

The second theme that needs reiteration is Suffering Servant, this time from the Christological perspective. The distinctive Christian message is, "A New Creation has occurred in human history, releasing into its processes and relationships a new kind of social energy that is both redemptive and fulfilling."[54] The Christ-event released energies that are redemptive that continue through history and a qualitative attainment that specifies the relationship of God toward humanity and humanity toward God. Again, the issue at the heart of Christology is power and goodness.

Christology makes a statement about how relationships are entered into by God. From the human perspective, power has been conceived of by its effects. Power can also mean the ability to receive an effect. Power that arises out of a sensitive regard for relationships can never be simply external force; and for that reason it will not be simply coercive. To have power without goodness is to seek effects without concern for the fact of relatedness; that is, to assert oneself with indifference to this fact of relatedness, or to turn this fact of relatedness to one's own interest and thus exploit relationships for the sake of one's autonomous ends.[55]

So too is this the case with God as revealed in Christ. Both transcendence and immanence are essential even to a limited and tentative formulation of the character of the living God. Otherwise, power without goodness, or goodness without power are degraded to the level of sheer sentimentality. Two routes out of the impasse are possible: metaphysical or Christological. The first, the metaphysical route is a view from the human perspective. The New Realism in metaphysics which Meland does attend to seeks to understand the meaning of internal relations from the empirical basis given by James. Meland states that metaphysical extensions of thought must be based in empirical facts or history. The ground for his own thinking in this area moves to the empiricism of the newer insights of realism based on human experience. In this context, the power of internal relations takes on a sensitivity toward

100

the mutuality of relations. Sensitivity becomes a form of power which accepts the relationships for what they are. Brute force even pales by the force of such power.

The second route is Christological. The task of Christology is to illumine God's participation in the concrete events of history which discloses His life, as being immanent as a redemptive and creative power, giving depth and new opportunities to people's lives. God becomes irrevocably qualified by the historic imagery of the Suffering Servant which is His revelation. Hence, the imagery of the Suffering Servant and its cultural importance for relationships expresses the nature of God as suffering love. For Meland, "process" thought through the critique of internal relations on the metaphysical level converges with the Christian revelation of God. The result is that God's power is qualified by His goodness and expressive of it.[56] The argument is a convergence of metaphysics and Christology which mutually help one another. Hence, in the concern for others who are looking for meaning in their lives, metaphysics leads to a possible faith in God. From the Christological side, the Christian believer need not fear the cultural dimensions of faith where God will be present. The challenge to the Christian is to live and witness faith everywhere. Both of these approaches ask for a sensitivity to the gentle working of God in the web of relations that is reality. In Christian faith, this sensitivity is the central proclamation of love. The individual opens up appreciatively toward this divine working when he accepts relationships already present and operative with "birth"—God, others, and self. The individual who believes encounters other centers of freedom forming a community of witness to the Christ event. This witness is greater when it is corporate, or cultic. As seen before, the sustaining nature of the spirit is done through a matrix which is the insertion of the individual back into the corporate context. The new life in the spirit "becomes an enduring depth of grace within the relationships that body forth the living Christ and his reconciling Word, in the decisions, acts, negotiations, response of men and women working at pertinent issues in society."[57] Here we have the seminal witness of the Church as a community becoming the body of Christ.

Conclusion

Christology under the New Realism has both a life of its own as the immanent statement about who God is for humanity and a source of faith which qualifies relationships, especially those of goodness and power. What falls under the New Realism in Meland's methodology of Empirical Realism is the manner of entering into the relationships. Not stated, yet present throughout the expression of Christology, is the role of the Appreciative Awareness. The sensitivity of relationships, for instance, where the ability to receive an effect is in the concrete terms of suffering love requires an openness to reality as relational on its own terms. The Appreciative Awareness does just that. The Rational Consciousness is not at stake. A new method of appraisal is what is needed which has come in the concept of the Appreciative Awareness.

One section, however, remains to complete the trinitarian understanding in Meland's theology.

Part 3: Holy Spirit

The third and only remaining topic to complete the Christian content of faith with respect to God is the Holy Spirit. In many ways, the theology of the Holy Spirit has been a minor theme. It remains subservient to the concept of God as Father and Jesus Christ. Under the New Realism, however, the emphasis of the Holy Spirit is important precisely because the methodology of Empirical Realism attends to the "More" of reality especially seen under such concepts as creativity and spirit. In a world where appearances are forms and symbols of the deeper dimension that is present, spirit is a crucial concept. In many ways, the role of God as Creative Passage in the world also partakes of this important human concept of spirit which is God's Spirit. In order to gain knowledge of the Holy Spirit, Empirical Realism begins with the experience of spirit.

The human person has a unique structure which is expressed as a dimension of depth. This depth expresses existence at its profoundest level coming out of the stream of life. Depth issues in freedom as a dimension of sensitivity in which we participate freely and consciously.[58] Meland describes it this way, "Spirit then is a given structure of being and sensitivity which awaits our participation in the creative ground of each actual self, imparting to it relationships which at once qualify and enhance its individuated self-experience and bringing to each self a visitation of judgment and grace."[59] The dimension of freedom on the first level which allows the individuation process to happen releases the functions of imagination, reverie, critical thought, and decision. This freedom is implicit in the human personality from the beginning. In a real way, it is the course of creative, rational, and moral experience. For Meland, this is an empirical statement of the human personality. On the second level, freedom allows the person to participate in the spontaneous and transcending acts of spirit. Here the person is not so much asserting his structure as responding to the lure of the sensitivity that adheres in the relations that form its creative context. Since both of these levels of freedom are really united, the person is drawn totally, with bodily feelings, the mind, and volitional responses, into the orbit of this freedom which is of the spirit. Meland calls this the "realm of spirit." At this second level, where conscious commitment in faith takes place, the Spirit of God is discerned.

Goodness in relationships is what Spirit promotes. This is not a product of human association which can be produced at will, or manipulated, or directed. Our conscious encounter with Spirit is spontaneous, intermittent, and of short duration. In some ways, these moments are akin to scientific insights of discovery. More appropriately, these occasions are encounters. They are more usually found in occasions of extremity; i.e., moments or situations which bring "a vivid awareness of our limits of selfhood, either through a sense of defeat, depletion, or despair, requiring the healing of forgiveness and a redemptive good; or through a heightening experience of appreciative awareness in which that which is not-self can be apprehended as in the I-Thou relationship."[60]

Spirit then connotes a depth of sensitivity that forms the matrix of relations in which all life is cast. It is a depth of sensitivity that is not so much known as lived in. Meland sees spirit as a kind of womb or matrix out of which the waking life of individual persons emerges and in which individuals participate whether knowingly or unknowingly. Meland says that "spirit is a quality of being which arises out of a particular depth of sensitivity in relations. It is a goodness in relationships."[61]

Despite the difficulty of expressing the dimension of spirit, nevertheless the Holy Spirit is real God.[62] Meland uses the legacy of Christian faith to help formulate the contemporary understanding under the new imagery. Christian language has traditionally used the term Holy Spirit as the immediate working of the concrete nature of God. The Spirit, for instance, expressed the working of God after the resurrection in the apostolic community. It would be correct to say that this discernible and apprehendable working of God in the Creative Passage is the Holy Spirit. In other words, the concrete nature of God is the Holy Spirit. The Holy Spirit is both independent of human manipulation and yet dependent upon the cooperation of human acceptance and sensibilities to allow the workings of God to be present. If the Holy Spirit is the discerned nature of God working in the ambiguity of human limitations, can the work of the Holy Spirit be distinguished from the work of Christ?

Meland understands the Spirit and Christ as integrally interrelated. Yet they are distinguishable in human events. Through what is an interesting and consistent extension of his methodology, Meland says that, first of all, the work of the Holy Spirit as the concrete nature of God is made possible by the work of Christ. Or, the revelation of God which enters forever into human life and history energizes the work of the Spirit. Secondly, the Spirit reaches people and transforms them "if not by reconstructing their conscious lives, at least by quickening their sense of sin, their awareness of a good not their own, and, possibly, by impelling them to an affection for this good that is of God."[63] The Christ thus becomes identified as the recreative or redemptive energy that is traceable within culture. The Holy Spirit is not this cultural mediation of redemptive energy. Rather, the Holy Spirit is the concrete working of God present in the immediacies of reality as the Creative Passage. The revelatory event of Christ continues as redemptive energy through the witness of faith: culture, cultus, and the individual. Through the myth and mythos of the scriptures, the Christ is present, alive today! These provide the conditions for the working of the Holy Spirit within human structures. The cooperation with the Holy Spirit is the direct and immediate interpenetration of the transcendent structure of faith. To a large extent, the sensitive perception on the part of the individual to the Spirit depends on the Appreciative Awareness. Meland explains the interpenetration this way: "Culturally speaking, this continuing redemptive energy preparing men to respond to the work of grace as a direct impartation of the Holy Spirit, is the living Christ within the social organism."[64] On the empirical side to which this points the being grasped by God through this depth of sensitivity as the communal ground of our existence is the Holy Spirit.[65] Jesus Christ, then, is the revealer of God and the mediator of God's redemptive work. Christ permeates culture as the recreative or redemptive energy; in part by symbolism of his life and work, in part by the sentiment in the Christian Community centered in him, and in part by the witness to him at all levels of human discourse.[66]

The depth of living creative of spirit depends upon the relations of reality. The role of the Appreciative Awareness under the New Realism discerns the influences of the relations. The depth of spirit in the human person can be encouraged, in the sense of deepened, or it can be blocked and stifled. The spirit of the person opens up to Spirit in an encounter with divine reality. When conscious commitment enters in, which orients the person toward the reality of Spirit, there is faith. Appreciative Awareness as a sensitive mode allows the working of the Christian legacy to identify religious experience as Christian.[67] Thus, the content of the legacy of faith with respect to God informs the Appreciative Awareness in its identification and discrimination. The role of the Appreciative Awareness remains at the heart of Meland's theology.

Between Faith and Appreciative Awareness

The trinitarian view of God identifies the legacy of faith as particularly Christian. The revelation of God which came in Christ has a witness which is the Church. The witness of the Church, moreover, bears witness to the revelation of God through itself (Cultus), the individuals, and the culture. The purpose of the witness is not content itself, but a living encounter with the reality of God. What happens when the person encounters God in some way is the issue of faith. In chapter two, I defined faith. In chapter three, the vortices of experience, or orbits of meaning, or witnesses of faith were explained in their integral connection with faith. The orbits are the Individual, the Culture, and the Cultus. Orbits in themselves did not present the content of the legacy of faith which identified a believer as Christian. The fourth chapter presented the distinctive revelation of God in the faith experience of the past and present. Chapters two, three, and four together present Meland's systematic presentation of faith under the methodology of Empirical Realism. Yet Meland's insights into the understanding of faith under Empirical Realism come from his understanding of the New Realism. As a reaction to Liberalism, the New Realism has insights that can help explain the legacy of faith and the relations involved. The precise tool for attending to context and relations is the Appreciative Awareness. This was chapter one.

As one would anticipate, there is a connection between the Appreciative Awareness and Faith. Just what the relationship is, has been obliquely indicated in spots. That the two concepts stand together to mutually inform one another is indubitable. We have seen the need for the Appreciative mode throughout the discussion of faith in all its various aspects. What then is the relationship between Appreciative Awareness and Faith? This is the next chapter.

CHAPTER IV

Part I

[1] FFS, p. xiii.

[2] FC, p. 112.

[3] Ibid., p. 91.

[4] Ibid.

[5] Ibid., p. 110.

[6] FFS, p. 151-2.

[7] Ibid., p. 151.

[8] Ibid., p. xiii.

[9] Ibid., p. xiv.

[10] Ibid.

[11] FC. Ibid., p. 100.

[12] FC, pp. 211-2.

[13] Ibid., p. 277.

[14] Ibid., p. 212.

[15] Ibid., p. 278.

[16] RF, p. 279.

[17] FFS, p. 81.

[18] Cf. Ibid., p. 146.

[19] FC, pp. 212-3.

[20] Ibid., p. 213.

[21] Ibid., p. 215.

[22] Ibid.

[23] Ibid.

[24] FFS, p. 142.

[25] FC, p. 215.

[26] FFS, p. 149.

[27] FC, p. 221.

[28] FFS, p. 72.

[29] RF, p. 265.

[30] Ibid., p. 279.

[31] Ibid., p. 267.

[32] The concept of power which complements Meland's view is given in Bernard Loomer, "Two Concepts of Power," *Process Studies*, vol. 6 (Spring, 1976), p. 5-32. Loomer's is a more thorough understanding of power from the relational point of view.

[33] RF, p. 283.

[34] FC, p. 200.

[35] Ibid., p. 201.

[36] Ibid., p. 202.

[37] RF, p. 217.

[38] There is an interesting similarity in the use of "mystery" as a positive statement about the nature of God between Meland and Karl Rahner. Though Meland is empirical and Rahner belongs to the Transcendental Thomist approach, I think that they both use the concept in similar ways.

Part 2.

[39] FFS, p. 159.

[40] FC, p. 86.

[41] Ibid., p. 197.

[42] Ibid., p. 198-9.

[43] Ibid., p. 199.

[44] Ibid.

[45] Ibid.

[46] RF, p. 181.

[47] Ibid., p. 181-2.

[48] Meland prefers "New Creation" as a biblical term to other uses such as Tillich's "New Being" which is not biblical.

[49] RF, p. 180.   Tillich uses "preparatory revelation" and Loomer uses "structures of particularity" which Meland likes.   These phrases probe the significance of the accumulative probability of response, a potential or incipient matrix of sensitivity consonant with the dimension of sensitive relations inherent and explicit in the New Creation.

[50] FFS, p. 101.

[51] Ibid., p. 78.

[52] Ibid., p. 81.

[53] RF, pp. 246-7.

[54] Ibid., p. 267.

[55] Cf. Ibid., Ch. 12.

[56] Ibid., pp. 278-9.

[57] Ibid., p. 261.

Part 3.

[58] Ibid., p. 232.

[59] Ibid., p. 234.

[60] Ibid., p. 235.

[61] Ibid., p. 234.

[62] FC, p. 216.

[63] Ibid., p. 217.

[64] Ibid., p. 218.

[65] RF, p. 227.

[66] FC, pp. 217-8.

[67] David Tracy makes the threefold distinction in experience as: (1) religious experience, (2) theistic experience, and (3) Christocentric experience. Meland is aware of the differences although he does not really make much use of the distinction between religious and theistic experience as categories. He is attuned to markedly Christian content experiences as his empirical use of Spirit indicates. Meland's empirical approach opens Tracy's approach to fuller expression. David Tracy, *Blessed Rage for Order.*

110

CHAPTER V

FAITH AND APPRECIATIVE AWARENESS

In this chapter, I will present the interrelationship of Faith and Appreciative Awareness. The first four chapters explained the basic concepts of each and how they operated. Their dependency upon one another has been explained. This chapter emphasizes the differences. Another way of saying this difference is: What can be attributed to Faith that cannot be attributed to the Appreciative Awareness? I will examine the Appreciative Awareness from the perspective of theological methodology so as to present the limits of appreciative inquiry with respect to faith. Then, with what I think is more at the heart of faith experience, I will present the difference between Faith and Appreciative Awareness from the dimension of spirit which is really continuous with the problem of knowledge indicated by the methodological inquiry. Finally, I will present the difference between Faith and Appreciative Awareness from what happens to the individual who in the classical sense of theology, "seeks understanding," from faith. This chapter concludes the relationships between Faith and Appreciative Awareness.

Theological Methodology

In the final book of his trilogy, *Fallible Forms and Symbols* (1976), Meland makes the best statement about his own reflection on method: "It may be commonplace to observe that reflection upon method often follows most productively upon engagement with an undertaking. There is a minimal amount of conscious design in what one undertakes initially in one's theological inquiry: enough, that is, to chart one's course of inquiry at that particular stage and to define one's procedure; but maturity in becoming self-conscious about what one has been doing generally follows as a view in retrospect."[1] What Meland has been insistent about through all three works is "the concern to see religious inquiry as being oriented simultaneously to the cultic and cultural experiences of a people, rather than being exclusively centered in the cultus of the historic church."[2] As a source of inquiry, this theological methodology springs from faith and remains faithful to it. For our purposes, the place of the Appreciative Awareness in this inquiry has a definite place and sequence.

Before moving into methodology, two points need to be mentioned. The first is that little secondary material on Bernard E. Meland has been writ-

111

ten. What has been done is not extensive. One work that has been done attempts to explain his methodology. This work by W.C. Peden in 1974 did not have Meland's final book available.[3] Peden did draw upon material both published and unpublished. Although much of Meland's method had been discussed elsewhere previous to 1976, not until his third book of the trilogy was published did the unity of the works become finalized. The best source for Meland's methodology comes from Meland himself. His article, not included in the trilogy, "How is Culture a Source for Theology,"[4] provides the best comprehensive view. This brings me to the second point. It is not my purpose to present a comprehensive explanation of method. By using both the article by Meland and the one on Meland by Peden, I want to present the conclusions in order to present the place and sequence of the Appreciative Awareness. Parenthetically, I would like to point out that there is a remarkable consistency in Meland's method that can be seen throughout the trilogy. It extends to other works after 1945 as well, when Meland's approach solidified into a uniform procedure.

Meland has four prolegomena to his theological method. The four prolegomena are followed by three steps. The Appreciative Awareness emerges in the three steps.

The first prolegomenon is: To gain a self-understanding of one's role as participant in a cultural faith.[5] This step includes the acknowledgement, as well as acceptance, of the limitations of the faith's historical witness. The emphasis rests upon the relationship between faith and culture.

The second prolegomenon is: An understanding of the relative situation in which each cultural witness stands. Remember, the word "relativity" under the New Realism contains the understanding that each perspective is partial and relates to the whole web-like structure of reality. The relativity of cultural faith, for instance, bears within its perspective a reference to ultimacy. In this instance, the witness of faith is not simply bound culturally, but possesses energy and spirit beyond itself. Meland's favorite phrase is that immediacies and ultimates traffic together. The obverse, as we have seen, is also true: faith cannot disregard the spirit's working in culture.

The third prolegomenon deals with myth which is an essential issue for Meland's theological position: An understanding of the phenomenon of myth in culture, and of the underlying mythos which shapes its orbit of meaning. Remember, myth is the response which a particular people makes to what is ultimate in their existence. Mythos is the elemental orbit of meaning in a culture which gives structure and direction at the level of the human psyche and within the realm of imaginative and cognitive experience. To participate in the mythos means that the person is responsive to what is ultimate within the context of his existence. People may become sophisticated to an extent and attempt to dissociate themselves from their mythos on the conscious and subconscious level. Since it is impossible to break with the mythos, the importance of coming to understand the phenomena of the myth and the underlying mythos is obvious.[6]

The fourth prolegomenon, which is a continuation from the third concerns the forms of participation in the mythos. Though not easily discernible in its various forms, three distinct clusters can be recognized: the Individual, the Cultus, and the Culture. Though Peden sees this as a fourth prolegomenon, Meland does not single it out but keeps it as a kind of transition to the three basic steps. The difference in these forms, however, should raise questions for theology: the relations between faith and culture, the individual and community, and tradition and present developing outlooks.

Peden has a summary of the thrust of Meland's prolegomena:

> The prolegomena to Meland's method indicate
> that his theology gives emphasis to the general theme of
> the relationship of faith and culture. The faith's histori-
> cal witness must be understood, especially in the light of
> the relative situation in which each cultural witness
> stands. This understanding requires a clear insight of the
> phenomenon of myth in the culture, and of the under-
> lying mythos which shapes its orbit of meaning. In order
> to deal with the mythos of any culture, one must have a
> working knowledge of the various forms of participation
> in the mythos.[7]

The reason that I quoted Peden's summary is that the role of the Appreciative Awareness is already expressed and anticipated. The "clear insight" of the understanding of myth and mythos can only come from the Appreciative Awareness and its perception of reality as open-ended yet with real limitations impinging upon the individual. What then are the three basic steps of Meland's theological method that are attentive to these prolegomena?

(1)   The first step is that the person encounters his absolute limit as a creature of the earth. In this encounter, faith occurs. The encounter itself is not faith; rather, God transforms the person in the encounter that issues in faith. As a "good not our own," faith is a redemptive gift orienting the person toward the future. The impact comes as a refocusing of the individual in faith. The encounter sensitizes one toward a new depth in the relationships of life. Meland designates this relationship as Appreciative Awareness. The Appreciative Awareness is first an aid to faith in the encounter and secondly a source of continued nurture for the future from the meaning of the encounter.

113

(2)   The second step is critical analysis. This step provides identification and discrimination once an encounter has happened. Critical analysis is important because it offers a discipline by which the person can become sensitive and open to the new depths of apprehension which has come as a disclosure. Critical analysis yields a richness to the experience of encounter and makes it possible to become sensitive toward the relational reality in which the person participates. In any theological method, the use of reason is important. The definition of theology is "faith seeking understanding." Critical analysis helps provide that understanding. Reason becomes transformed by faith as to the specific focus of the person's attention. Reason then becomes recreative and redirected by faith toward the reality of God. Reason then aids the deepening of faith.

Step one has had the primacy of faith its interest. Step two has had the critical and analytical aspect of faith its interest.

(3)   The third step is that the theologian must consider seriously the historical and communal witness to the Christian faith expressed in the revelation of Christ. It is, after all, the revelation of God in Christ that marks belief as "Christian." One need not jump to this center of Christian witness immediately. But some time, critical analysis must confront seriously the biblical and communal witness. This means that a creative encounter with the gospel of judgment and grace from Scripture must be attended to in order to be Christian in the fullest sense, and includes our being instructed by the disciplined analysis and findings of critical biblical study. It also means that one's faith is not simply private and individual, but relational and communal. Especially in a Constructive Theology, it is necessary for the individual experience to confront and to converse with the communal witness of faith.

In the second step (critical analysis), Meland wants to take adequate measure of the relative situation in which each cultural witness stands. For the purpose of uniting Meland's method with his imagery in order to present as complete a schematic diagram as possible, I would like to use a quote from Meland which I think completes the notion of methodology. Meland notes his basic interest:

> To recognize that, while the life of every man is seen to
> be ambiguous by reason of his creaturely and cultural
> limitations, it is at the same time borne forth by, and in
> its daily moment of existence is impelled to bear witness
> to, an ultimate depth of reality. To my knowledge, Radi-
> cal Empiricism was the first metaphysical interpretation
> of human existence in the West to lift up the simul-
> taneous presence of an ultimate dimension of reality and
> the humanly imposed immediacies within the stream of

experience. Almost a generation before Existentialism and Phenomenology had become household words in the theological and philosophical vocabulary, Radical Empiricists were reacting against the abstractness of Hegelian idealism insisting upon taking human existence seriously both in its concrete immediacies and in the depth of its participation in this ultimate dimension of reality.

The basic imagery of my thought, following from this orientation of Radical Empiricism (which I have since come to speak of as Empirical Realism) presents existence in this two fold manner, as embracing simultaneously dimensions of immediacy and ultimacy.[8]

In summary, the empirical character of the individual is taken seriously, that a person lives within and by the faculties of his own organism. In addition, the faculties are attuned to reality so as to deal with it, but not without discipline and critical use. At the same time, the communal character is taken into consideration, that life is organic, relations are real, and reality is social with energies operative in culture today. Relationships are creative in the tensions that they bring. Growth towards meaning takes place and the spirit is unleashed through these structures of experience. The spirit is sustained by growth toward community. God gives direction to this evolving structure of experience through the Creative Passage. Meland tries to hold the primary relationships together. Faith is at the bottom of any theological foundation and therefore a primary relationship of the person to God. As primary, Meland presupposes faith before he elaborates his method. This is crucial to Meland's method and to the use of the Appreciative Awareness.

Appreciative Awareness in the method of Meland provides a focus to one-already-believing. Or, the Appreciative Awareness receives focus through faith. It is not that the Appreciative Awareness does not orient the person to appreciate any number of different experiences, it does. But when the appreciative mode relates to faith, an encountered reality in faith finds the appreciative mode as an aid to perceiving and nurturing the individual's life and meaning. In the same way, the appreciative mode contributes to the communal witness, the cultural witness, and the cultic witness.

In effect, the appreciative mode states that experience is richer, deeper, and more pervasive than we give it credit. Critical reflection as the rational mode of consciousness cannot substitute for elemental or creatural presence to reality. Nor can critical reflection distill experience sufficiently. The appreciative mode allows for knowledge and understanding and a presence toward reality unlike the rational mode. It is as if the appreciative mode "expanded" reality for the individual as wider, deeper, richer, and more

115

pervasive.

The question of method is one of inquiry and procedure. With faith presupposed for the method, the place of Appreciative Awareness comes as a focus for the encounter that issues in faith. The question, in part, is one of knowledge. Method deals with the process of "seeking understanding." Another dimension of the relationship between faith and Appreciative Awareness is the source of the encounter itself which is at the basis of the methodological considerations. Let us turn to the encounter itself as an expression of the Spirit to gain another perspective on the relationship between Faith and Appreciative Awareness.

The Spirit, Appreciative Awareness and Faith

What we meet in an I-Thou encounter is not two structures of experience but the reality of unique centers of freedom. The reality is what impels, transforms, overtakes us.[9] What we know of spirit is what we can empirically grasp in these intermittent occasions of sensitive encounter.[10] Spirit, in a general sense, means "a transcendent quality or movement of grace which has its source in God."[11] The perception of spirit presents the relationship between Faith and Appreciative Awareness from its empirical source in human experience. Meland points out, "This amounts to designating the sense in which man, in his behavior, attitude, or character actually transcends himself as a structure, actually becomes the bearer of meaning which can be called a good not his own."[12]

The most elemental expression of spirit in the human creature for Meland is the sense of wonder. The definition of wonder is: "the spontaneous play of thought not focused by any functional purpose."[13] Indicative of the spiritual dimension, Meland distinguishes three stages in wonder: (1) Open Awareness; (2) Appreciative Awareness; and (3) Creative Awareness. Wonder is a continuous response but these stages indicate degrees of receptiveness, integration, and conscious response which adds both discipline and directive effort to the individual. The process proceeds as follows:

(1)   Open Awareness is receptiveness to the full datum of experience. The structure of any living creature, whether individual or organized, seems to work against this open awareness. Take, for example, the process of Individuation which brings the individual's concerns toward the self in order to grow and reinsert the individual back into relations. Thus, open awareness is never quite an actuality in human response but a condition sought. The point is that there must be a sense of wonder or the person becomes closed within structural barriers.

(2)   Appreciative Awareness connotes a more positive expression of the

sense of wonder than sheer open awareness: "It implies further an open awareness toward the end of *knowing* the reality *out there* to its own right."[14] This step is specifically directed against all types of closures by the mind. It understands the mind, the feelings, the senses as interrelated with reality. Appreciative Awareness can become part of the habitual pattern of response, in which case, instead of closing the personality, maturation in the process of Individuation actually heightens the degree and discipline of Appreciative Awareness.

(3)   Creative Awareness means wonder becoming a creative force. The person directs the self toward participating in the creative forces at work. Even though the line between this stage and Appreciative Awareness (2) is slight, the appreciative capacity becomes a form of energy affecting the structure of relations that define the whole context of living in which this individual participates as a person.   For example, love then becomes a social energy of creative power and can be translated into civic and political energies.[15]   The Creative Awareness awaits the freedom of the individual to act and participate in spirit. Meland uses a descriptive phrase "the pitch of the organism," "bent," and "thrust toward the future" by which the human being reaches toward its new level of emergence, or "man moving toward his fruition at the level of the spirit."[16]

The three stages of wonder indicative of the spirit move toward greater appreciation that issues in increased capacity for decision. "Freedom is awareness of possibilities and a capacity to respond to them selectively."[17] Decision is the elimination of possibilities and the assertion of one direction of actuality. As Meland states, "Whatever enriches the act of decision through appreciative awareness, through sympathy, and the critical understanding of possibilities, aids man's capacity for freedom; and to that extent provides conditions for the emergence of spirit."[18]

Both freedom and wonder as expressive of spirit are crucial to faith. For faith in the transcendent aspect is a conscious commitment in love to the reality of God. Appreciative Awareness is conceptually isolated as one step in this process.   What is important for us is that the appreciative mode contributes to the life of faith.   Even from the perspective of spirit, appreciative awareness is focused by faith. The Appreciative Awareness serves faith by allowing the individual contact with reality experienced as deeper, wider, richer, and more pervasive than Rational Consciousness. In fact, the entire person is involved in the appreciative mode much the same as the entire person is involved in the commitment by the person to the reality of God encountered in experience. In other words, faith provides the orientation toward which the appreciative mode becomes sensitive. And although the possibility of illusion remains, critical reflection and the historical legacy of faith provide support to reduce the probability of illusion.

Wonder is not the only expression of spirit from which the Appreciative Awareness can be seen in its relation to faith, although it does seem to have a pre-eminence. Joy and Sorrow are grounded in Appreciative Awareness. Meland says, "It [Joy] is not concerned with egoistic satisfaction, but with participation in the actual goods of life, a giving of oneself to the appreciable meanings within experience."[19] Sorrow is an appreciative response in the same sense that joy is. Sorrow participates in real losses, ruptures of relations, and death. Meland says, "Noticing these instances of spirit in the human situation is always a matter of pointing, of appreciating, of enjoying, or of sorrowing."[20] The spirit itself may not be directly sought or self-consciously contained. It is given to a person out of relationships that have oriented that person to its good. The most mature orientation of the person toward ultimate meaning and reality is done in the act of faith. Faith, indeed, is the relationship grasped from the human side.

Meland notes that Spirit is not a sustained feature in the human creature. When it appears, it is ambiguously intermingled with complex counter tendencies. This ambiguity results in both the problem of good and the problem of evil. Yet, throughout the human life, there is a degree of spontaneity seen in acts of repentance, forgiveness, wonder, freedom, community, joy, and sorrow that point beyond the more visibly structured responses of the Moral and Rational Consciousness. A more marked degree of sensitivity and concern appear in these human responses suggesting the play of affections and the sensibilities that belong more properly to what is called the Appreciative Consciousness. Appreciative Consciousness serves faith's orientation to the reality of spirit. And, although it would seem most fruitful to explore and test the operations of the spirit in heightened and poignant moments, perhaps what might be called "peak experiences," these moments escape on-the-spot analytical inquiry. For it is the person who confronts the reality of spirit, and not the mind. Therefore faith asks the Appreciative Awareness to sharpen the perceptions in order to notice the occurrences of spirit and to quicken a zest to attend to its dynamic and creative happening, even participate in it. It is also true that Appreciative Awareness as a generalized attentiveness needs the sensitivity provided by the biblical witness, culture, and tradition. The content of faith, in other words, is extremely important to the focus of the Appreciative Awareness through faith. Hopefully, what will occur is a quality of response by the person which renders him more sensible to the emerging operation. To do so would require taking the covental experience seriously that God is related inextricably with humanity.

The contours of the relationship of Appreciative Awareness and Faith have been sketched from a methodological perspective integral to theological investigation, and from the realm of spirit expressed in the human response of wonder. Each one of these isolates the role of Appreciative Awareness as focused by faith: the first in terms of knowledge, the second in terms of encountered spirit. Although both viewpoints single out differences between Faith and Appreciative Awareness, the most marked distinction comes in the contribution that each one makes to the individual. This is the third perspective.

Knowledge and Love

Both Faith and Appreciative Awareness resemble one another in their function. For example, both Faith and Appreciative Awareness depend on trust. Meland says about Appreciative Awareness: "It offers a counter-movement in the mind which serves to temper or restrain the egoistic element in all intellectual effort."[21] And about Faith: "Faith, then we can say, is the precondition of thinking upon ultimate matters which gives some assurance of getting beyond the structural limitations of the thinking ego."[22] One way of distinguishing both Faith and Appreciative Awareness is in the results they bring. In other words, faith and the appreciative mode serve the individual in two different ways. What then are the end-products of faith and Appreciative Awareness?

Most fundamentally, the Appreciative Awareness is an organizing principle of the mind. Its functions with the Rational and Moral Consciousness. The Appreciative Awareness orients the person toward reality so that no preconceived limits are imposed by the individual upon reality. As an attitude, it attempts to allow the relationships of our creatureliness to impinge upon us. It involves a total presence by the individual participating in the awareness. As an aesthetic mode, an emphasis upon the sensing and feeling dimension is imperative. The feeling dimension undergoes critical analysis in the process of discrimination and identification. If asked what eventually results from this open attitude, the answer is knowledge. Granted that this knowledge is almost totally involving, based on trust, and involved in the richer, thicker "More" of reality that is not seen or distilled, the result is still knowledge.

Faith, most fundamentally, issues from an encounter empirically expressed as "a goodness not our own." Faith orients the person toward the ultimate reality expressed as goodness. As well, faith unleashes redemptive, psychic, and social energies. They are creative of the person in his relation toward reality to participate in the creative level of spirit. Faith requires a conscious commitment in freedom toward the God who is encountered. The relationship is that of an I-Thou relationshp where two centers of freedom meet. The central fact of goodness and forgiveness is expressed in the relationship of love. Whereas the Appreciative Awareness ends in knowledge, faith ends in love.

Meland identifies the Protestant effort as a movement to awaken a religious affection that would transfer the lives of men and women from the orbit of themselves to the orbit of God. Meland makes a poignant statement that drives to the heart of the problem:

> The sense of a good not our own, yet imperative to our good as a never-failing source of grace and judgment, is precisely the feeling-tone that will awaken the affective regions of consciousness. The Protestant appeal to faith rests upon the *knowledge of Christ,* not as philosophic reflection derives knowledge but as the total nature of man, his appreciative and affective powers together with thought, *discerns* the redemptive good of experience disclosed in sacrificial love.[23]

Faith orients the person in love. Faith and love are inextricable in the Christain response. The invitation to enter into the relationshp with God is given precisely as gift. The gift of God Himself in the encounter elicits the response of the individual in love, characterized by faith. The invitation to this conventional relationshp is total and requires a commitment by the individual which includes the appreciative powers. Love becomes the culmination of the process of growth and development. It would be true to say that faith therefore brings the Appreciative Awareness to the service of love. Love requires the nurture and sensitivity that the appreciative mode delivers. Love becomes richer, deeper, and more sensitive. At the same time there is a definite focus for love, such that suffering love might be required. In like manner, the love of God toward humanity has a focus such that God is revealed as involved with humanity to the extent of suffering love. The central symbol of love which extends even to suffering for another expresses God's relationship towards us and calls forth from us the quality of love that we should have for God and others.

The matrix of relationships does not escape the judgment of grace and redemption. All relationships are governed by love. There can be no severing of love from relationships without killing the religious affections of the person. Called to love, everything that is done comes under the command of love—or in the negative expression, nothing, no relationship, can exceed love's demands. And the quality of the love relationship, which is Faith's endproduct, can be enhanced by the appreciative mode which opens the person to a richer, thicker, "More" or reality. Love becomes deeper, richer, thicker, more pervasive, and perhaps suffering as well. In the process, the Spirit emerges and sustains that love relationship such that the person more deeply involves the self in the reality of self, of others, and of God.

Conclusion

There is an integral relationship between Faith and Appreciative Awareness. Both of them orient the person toward a "More" of reality beyond the Rational Consciousness. Far from being incompatible, the Rational, Moral, and Appreciative Consciousnesses complement one another. Together they aid the individual to perceive and respond to reality. When reality comes as a personal encounter with love, initiating commitment by the individual in love to continue and develop the relationship, faith emerges. Faith certainly comes as a gift, of grace and judgment, and as recreative of the individual socially and psychically. Faith orients the person in other words. Part and parcel of the orientation is the nurture that comes from human powers to sense, perceive, feel, think, and judge. Faith serves to present the reality of God encountered to the powers of the individual. In this way, faith focuses appreciative awareness. At the same time, Appreciative Awareness serves faith. Meland says, "Faith as appreciative awareness, unattended by critical intrusion, is the art of human response to the abundance of meaning in the datum that is of ultimate concern to the creatural experience and to all existence. It is the thrust of the creature toward the source of his creaturehood in an effort to nullify as far as possible the limiting effects of his own creatureliness."[24]

Appreciative Awareness is very much an "art." As Meland developed in our first chapter, it has a method of its own. It is a skilled response that becomes better through disciplined effort. It is akin to the museum goer who moves from "looking" at pictures to an "appreciation" of them. Communication from painter to perceiver takes place and allows the perceiver to experience a wider, deeper, richer, and more pervasive reality than mere "looking." But the ability to appreciate comes with discipline and time, and depends on the powers of the human being to continue to develop the skills necessary.

Faith uses appreciative skills to put the person in relation to the reality of God. If faith is presupposed to the method, the appreciative skills nurture the person to deepen what faith asks, and that is to love. Appreciative skills cannot take the place of faith. Faith depends upon the appreciative awareness for the nurturing of love and the deepening of our sensibilities and knowledge of the love relationship. Appreciative awareness presents the person with understanding of the creatural limitations and relations that are part of the reality within which we are bound and from which we possess our strength.

121

Summary

The concept of Appreciative Awareness (Chapter I) has an important relationship to Faith in the thought of Bernard E. Meland. The relationship demanded an explanation of Faith (Chapter II). The function of faith and its dependency upon the Appreciative Awareness includes the witnesses of faith understood as the Individual, the Culture, and the Cultus (Chapter III). No explanation, however, could avoid the content of faith as the reality encountered. The content most clearly depends upon the understanding of God, Jesus Christ, and the Holy Spirit (Chapter IV). In many ways, the integral relationship of Appreciative Awareness to Faith existed throughout the explanation of faith. The explanation and topics of faith depend upon the Appreciative Awareness. As a matter of fact, Faith in Meland's theology is incomprehensible without Appreciative Awareness. What needed to be done in the fifth chapter was present the underlying differences so that the function of each could be clearly defined. Three approaches to the differences between faith and Appreciative Awareness come in the methodology, the encounter, and the end-product of each orientation.

Methodology served to locate the appreciative mode in the act of inquiry. As Meland says, "Faith and inquiry become two inseparable rhythms which continually alternate in the course of human experience."[25] Appreciative Awareness emerged as a focus to faith which is presupposed in the method, and makes the method truly theological. Methodology, however, presents an ordered pattern of inquiry. What about the encounter itself? The second approach dealt with the emergence of spirit. Perhaps the best example of transcending spirit occurs in wonder. Again, the process of wonder used the appreciative mode as a focus for emerging spirit. The third approach separated out what both Appreciative Awareness and Faith focus the individual towards. In the case of Appreciative Awareness, the end-product is knowledge that involves the total person. In the case of faith, the end-product is love which is a total response by the individual-in-relationship-with-God. Whatever the various form faith takes, whether as appreciative, as understanding, as content, as inquiry, as commitment—they all lead the individual to the love relationship with God. The nurture of faith is the nurture of love. Love is inextricable to faith and the appreciative mode serves faith. The end-product of Faith and Appreciative Awareness most clearly distinguishes the difference between them.

The full circle has been completed. The interrelationshp of Faith and Appreciative Awareness so integral to Meland's theology has been explained. This brings to an end the formal discussion of Faith and Appreciative Awareness. What remains to be done is an evaluation.

NOTES

CHAPTER V

[1] FFS, p. xv.

[2] Ibid.

[3] W. C. Peden, "Meland's Philosophical Method—Part one," *Iliff Review*, 3 (Spring, 1974), 43–53; "Part Two," (Fall, 1974), 34–35.

[4] "How Is Culture a Source for Theology," *Criterion* 3 (1964), 10–21.

[5] Meland says much of the same formulation in "How is Culture. . . ." and I will use Peden's formulation which is correct. I do disagree with Peden's use of Meland's "philosophical method." I see no justification for this. Since Meland relies upon faith as a beginning point, "theological method" might be more justified. Also cf. Philip Hefner, "Theological Worldliness: Bernard Meland's Contribution to Theological Methodology," *Quest* 8 (1964), 26–32.

[6] Ibid., p. 45.

[7] Ibid., p. 46.

[8] Meland, "How Is Culture. . . ," p. 11.

[9] RF, p. 227.

[10] Ibid., p. 226.

[11] FC, p. 171.

[12] Ibid., p. 172.

[13] Ibid. Also see C.S. Peirce's "Musement."

[14] Ibid., p. 174.

[15] Ibid., p. 175.

[16] Ibid.

[17] Ibid.

[18] Ibid., p. 177.

[19] Ibid., p. 180.

[20] Ibid., p. 183-4. Liberation theology expressed by Jon Sobrino has a similar use of sorrow which makes for an interesting comparison. *Christology at the Crossroads*, pp. 199-201. The role of suffering also becomes a concern for Faith and Appreciative Awareness. There is affinity between Meland and Schillebeeckx who in *Christ: The Experience of Jesus as Lord* (New York: Seabury Press, 1980) presents suffering as a common human experience from which salvation enters (pp. 646-839). In what would be an interesting development of the Appreciative Awareness, a negative insight or lack of appreciation of suffering in itself would be the first step toward an openness to God's salvific work and give methodological impetus to Schillebeeckx's experiential approach.

[21] Ibid., p. 118.

[22] Ibid., p. 123.

[23] One need not claim this simply for Protestantism. The claim of faith can be claimed throughout the tradition of Catholicism. For instance, Ignatius of Loyola claimed as much in the era of the Reformation in his *Spiritual Exercises*, second week, third prelude. More will be said about this possible comparison in the CONSIDERATIONS.

[24] FC, p. 120.

[25] Ibid., p. vii.

CONSIDERATIONS

Many limitations beset a student. Not an inconsiderable one becomes wrestling with the self. It is not unlike Jacob's wrestling with the angel. What seemed a fair and even match at the start, ended with Jacob's humanity unfairly used against him: a dislocated hip! The moral is to know one's limitations and what one is getting in for. But, alas, knowledge comes with struggle and limitations emerge only when one is vulnerable and wrestles. The attempt to appropriate another person's thoughts, feel as he does, and present those insights faithfully brings the student into confrontation with his limitations. The inability to say everything at once, but only one plodding sentence after another, was summed up by a friend of mine who reminded me: "God made time so that everything doesn't happen at once!" And as tumbling wrestlers sometimes do, it was difficult at times to separate who was speaking: Meland or Mueller. Some attempt to distinguish the two has to be made. Since my own limitations depend upon the considerations of others, I would like to make a few considerations on Meland's works. These "considerations" attempt to locate some of the limits of Meland's works and present a few possibilities for development.

1.   There exists in Meland's work a problem with language. Critics and reviewers of Meland's works have pointed this out. I also found difficulty with the language myself. There are reasons for the problem as I have come to understand Meland better. At least one of the problems involved with the language usage is the reliance upon so-called "process" philosophy—typified especially by Alfred North Whitehead. Whitehead developed a new vocabulary to deal with his philosophy of organism. Meland understands and employs these concepts in his own thought. Meland does not hesitate to take exception to Whitehead's vocabulary and to use his own theological formulations. Thus, those not familiar with process vocabulary will have initial difficulty with Meland's thoughts. But I think this problem of parallel concepts to process vocabulary is not a major difficulty because Meland takes pains to not let the vocabulary come in the way of the thought. David Hall represents one wing of the criticism of language but sees it this way: "Meland is more successful than anyone writing today—theologian or philosopher—in distilling the essence of process thinking from the dross of its technical vocabulary without sacrificing the uniqueness and power of that sensibility."[1] I think that this is true. At the same time, there is a wing of criticism which finds Meland's vocabulary too obscure and imprecise.[2] I think that there is truth here too. From my own reading, I found Meland's language descriptive and poetic at times when I preferred precision and clarity. It must be pointed out that there is a shift from book to book in the precision and clarity of concepts. In general, Meland becomes clearer and more definite in his terms in *Fallible Forms and Symbols*. His first work, *Faith and Culture*, seemed less clarified. To this extent, the third volume is a welcomed addition to the earlier ones.

To stay with this point for a moment, there is a qualitative difference between *Faith and Culture* and *Fallible Forms and Symbols*. I find *Faith and Culture* the most creative. It bursts with fresh insight, rawer enthusiasm, and has that quality of creativity of one caught up with possibilities and newness. Meland concurs that he considered this his best work, and I agree. Meland thought *Fallible Forms and Symbols* was also good; I would agree and rank it second. But *Fallible Forms and Symbols* is a different type of book: more reflective, clarifying, and having the characteristics of a maturer perspective which probes earlier thoughts. I found myself going to it for clarification.

Continuing with the problem of language, the initial obscurity that I encountered in places finally gave way in a break-through point after I had read the entire trilogy as well as other articles. My own question has been: What is the problem with the language?

My own reflection is that the words very closely mirror Meland's own method. Or, Meland's use of language reflects his method. By that I mean Meland, in his method, will not sacrifice the appreciative dimension for the rational. Rational clarity of definition is not the most important criterion of language. In poetry, for instance, meter and a word's descriptive quality must be considered. Language itself is relational. Meland deals with the difficult arena of ultimacy in cultural immediacies. What the reader deals with is most appropriately expressed by the art historian Jane Dillenberger:

> In making an analysis of painting or sculpture, we are compelled to verbalize that for which there is no verbal counterpart. Language must be probing and pointing rather than definitive. Most important of all, the language must focus on the work of art itself, rather than on ideas about the work of art. It must compel the reader to become a viewer. It is only after the long searching of the painting in and for itself that further interpretation can be indulged in without violating the work of art as a work of art.[3]

The relationship that Meland involves the reader with is that of a feeling, an appreciation, an acknowledgement. It is a method of "probing," and "pointing," in the manner of a disclosure so that the reader experiences what Meland says. The reader is asked to accept the articulation by Meland as true and representative of his experience. It is not a "definitive" logic. It compels "the reader to become a viewer." The focus must be on "the work of art itself," or in Meland's case, the relational reality of experience taken seriously. Whitehead's phrase "We think with our bodies" is most expressive of Meland's relational use of language. In many ways, Meland's poetic, descriptive component to language can be expected. Meland is both an artistic theologian and a theological artist.

I think the problem of language will be raised again and again. I think that the nature of what he has done leaves him open to that criticism and perhaps has accounted in part for his not having as wide a popular acceptance as I think he deserves. It is also to the point to say that Meland's works are experiencing a resurgence today. They seem to be more readable, or perhaps accepted, today than they were in the case of *Faith and Culture* when it first came out in 1953. There may be a development in our culture where his insights are more readily grasped, the appreciative dimension sought after, and his lanugage less threatening and obscure. Certainly Meland's third volume has added to the clarity by probing more of the presuppositions at work in his thought and which logically precede his first work of twenty-five years before.

The problem of language, I might add, is what prompted me to include a glossary. I think that the basic terminology is not that difficult. It needs to be collected for reference for those who do not have the time to read the entire trilogy for the "break through" but who want to come to a deeper appreciation of what Meland has to offer. Therefore, the language need not be a detriment but an enjoyment of the insights Meland has to offer.

2.   In addition to the aesthetic style, there is a corresponding existential character as to what prompts Meland to write. His theology responds to many demands even within one book. The approach seems to be more topical and allows for more themes to be woven into his works. Whereas Meland has been criticized for a kind of "looseness" to his books, Meland himself prefers to view the same quality as "existential." In line with his relational-contextual method, any topic is a starting point for relating with other topics. The movement which accepts the principle of relativity seriously allows for a type of weaving together of the whole. This appreciative approach is opposed to logical, iron-clad unity. At various times, in various stages of development, and depending upon the initial topic, the entire perspective changes and other related themes become important. The Jamesian "More" of reality allows for many various approaches at different times. The result is a coherence to Meland's thought as a whole which does not sacrifice his freedom of development and expression. At the same time, however, it is necessary to require at

some time a more penetrating analytical explanation. The analytical presentations of themes such as God, relations, faith, culture, and many others could provide a depth of understanding and sensitivity for the appreciative consciousness by way of the rational consciousness. Width and Depth must be correlated for the appreciative dimension to flourish.

One other consideration emerges over the sustained writing contained in article form. There is a better presentation for the reader of the development of Meland's thought. Meland himself changes over the twenty-five year period of writing the trilogy. Words that meant something to him originally either become more significant or less significant. Originally, the word "appreciative" came from artistic appreciation. Later it developed into the "textured character of reality." Likewise, "Creative Passage" was not as important in his early work as it was in his later one. Part of the reason for the importance of the Creative Passage later was the inadequacy of Meland to explain the meaning of God to his own satisfaction. Meland told me, for instance, that he removed a section on "God" that he had intended to publish in *Fallible Forms and Symbols*. Hence, the importance of the empirical understanding of God associated with the Creative Passage became more important as the explanation of God's relationships with the world. "Creative Interchange" on the other hand which was one early way of expressing his understanding of God gave way in his later work to the singular and categorical use of the Creative Passage. Even with the changes in Meland himself in his explanations, the trilogy has a remarkable consistency in the usage of language. Only slight shades of emphasis changed which traces the development of Meland himself.

3.   Meland indicates in the trilogy that his is a theology of culture. Since this is the case, it is not fair to expect every dimension of the faith experience to be examined. Nevertheless, the limits of Meland's thought might be pointed out for possible developments of faith which do not include this perspective.

It is interesting that for all the influence and importance that James exerted on Meland's thought, Meland never took the direction James indicated. James found the nature of religious conversion as irreducibly significant to knowledge and life.[4] Meland does not deal with religious conversion at all. For the most part, Meland begins his theology with faith presupposed. Meland also investigates the nature of ultimacy in experience, but not in individual conversion. It is also true to say that Meland deals with the ultimacy in reality toward which faith orients the person, but, again, conversion is not considered. Meland moves easily to the cultural dimension of faith in its social context with its energies and legacy. This is Constructive Theology for him. What remains open for further investigation then is the personal conversion process. Bernard Lonergan in his *Method* speaks about the need for conversion of the person on the intellectual, moral and religious levels. Using this frame of reference, Meland emphasizes the affective dimension of conversion through an intellectual conversion. Both work together for the total conversion of the person. Wherever the process of conversion begins, the remaining levels will have to undergo conversion eventually. Hence, Meland's intellectual assault on the affective dimension is acceptable. Meland is not interested in the moral or intellectual conversion as such. It is fair to say that Meland does not attend to them because of their emphasis in the Liberal tradition. Religious conversion is not the primary concern either, even though it does have a clear relationship to Meland's thought. For the Religious conversion in the modern world will have to explore the realm of the secular. Meland offers a clear linkage between the religious conversion and secular experience of ultimacy and the energies of faith. The objection could be directed against Meland that he needs a more complete understanding of the personal conversion process. Developmental psychology has prepared some ground here by the examination of the values involved in personal growth. Erikson and Piaget have provided a framework for such analysis.[5] In moral developmental theory, Kolberg has offered a similar frame of reference.[6] Of late, their work is beginning to spawn efforts in personal faith developments as the work of Fowler indicates.[7] All of these developmental approaches complement Meland's work and in some ways are grounded by Meland in his analysis of imagery and culture. Meland's direction is more contextual than personal and will therefore remain a constant challenge to personal, developmental theories that they should take the cultural context seriously.

Through the shrinking of distances between cultures, Meland has presented an understanding of culture, especially the Western culture, which can confront and learn from other cultures. Meland offers a confidence and trust beyond the culture to the workings of God in Christian faith. More than ever before, Christianity confronts strong divergent traditions of religious myths and with an appreciation for the values inherent in those cultures. Such a perspective is respectful of God's presence already at work. Meland has been ahead of his time in his concern for trans-cultural understanding of ultimacy.

4.   More than any other single factor, I am impressed by what I would call Meland's perspective. I call it a contextual-relational balance of tensions. In many ways, it is a correlational approach, but not in Tillich's sense of existential questions and Christian answers. Meland's correlational approach through the Appreciative Awareness is a mutual influencing, open to possibilities without undue presuppositions. Meland's correlation is relativity taken seriously where the starting point is relative and is related inextricably to the web-like structure of reality. The theory of relativity does have primary relationships for Meland. Meland's perspective is also one of faith. Faith's focus of the Appreciative Awareness allows access to reality different

from rational and moral modes, and therefore the appreciative approach to faith is a constitutive dimension of the person's relation to reality. Meland then both reads the culture and remains faithful to the Christian legacy. Meland sees tradition as a dynamic process which takes specific cultural forms. Meland also understands history's relation to theology as a dynamic one. In many ways, the transition to modern theology results from taking history seriously, which he does. What Meland lacks in modern theology is the new use of biblical criticism. Like many of his time, Meland does not have a hermeneutics by which he explains the development of the original Christian myth to its interpretation today. Recent biblical criticism has challenged every theologian's use of scripture.[8] There must be a justification for the use of scripture as consonant with the coherent exegesis that biblical criticism demands. For instance, is the Suffering Servant the best expression of Christ's revelation of the Father? If so, on what grounds can it be justified? To avoid random and personal use of the scripture as so many examples, the usage of Scripture must be justified by coherence and adequacy to biblical criticism.

5.   Although the appreciative element of faith is one of Meland's best insights and explanations, little has been done on it. One of Meland's achievements in the appreciative understanding of faith is the presentation of some correctives as to whether it operates correctly or not. In other words, Meland is not content to let feelings and emotions run independently of critical reflection. The total person is involved in a commitment of faith. Critical reflection dares not enter into the moment of appreciative awareness or else the moment makes a qualitative change to the rational mode. The analogy continually brought back by Meland is that of the artist or one developing art appreciation. Meland's three-step method of openness, identification, and discrimination might be explained in more critical ways. At least it is open to further clarification. I think one such handle might be provided by a set of questions. For instance, just as the rational and moral mode ask questions, critical reflection about the appreciative dimension can ask questions that the rational and moral consciousness cannot answer. For example, the moral consciousness responds to questions like: Is it right or wrong? The question is rational, but the answer is dependent upon the moral consciousness of the total person. The rational consciousness can ask questions such as: What is it? What does it mean? Its answers are clarifying and come from the total experience. Its ability is analytical and logical. Whitehead's phrase which Meland likes applies to these questions: "We think with our bodies." The rational mode does not preclude experiential modes. The appreciative consciousness might also respond to a battery of questions such as: Am I holy? Am I happy? Am I allowing myself to be open and influenced by my past? by others? by my self? What is the quality of my living? It would seem that if the appreciative mode is a skill which can be developed, then reflection through such types of questions as these might help to develop and hone the skill. Questions such as these would sensitize and direct the attention of the appreciative conscious-

ness. In this sense appreciative is vectoral. As vectoral, the appreciative mode does not control the data but remains open to the relationships themselves. In the same way as an art critic disciplines and deepens the human appreciation of art, the person can deepen one's appreciation of life's living.

6.   One of the presuppositions in Meland's own work which colors his perspective is his own background in American Protestant tradition. Certainly everyone begins from his own experience. The question becomes whether that experience is inclusive or exclusive of others' experiences. I cannot speak for other traditions, my limitation comes from my American Catholic background. But I can say that Meland's explanations have an inclusive quality about them. My background leads me to various intersections with Meland's. Today, it is becoming clearer that many of the differences between Protestant and Catholic America were magnified out of proportion because of their common tradition. Only recently have we come to see that Catholics and Protestants in America have understood themselves precisely in relation and contradistinction to one another. A type of give and take took place in their mutual developments which gave identity and took identity from each other. Today, in the wake of tremendous worldwide cultural upheaval, Protestant and Catholic distinctions look remarkably similar. In the face of other strong religious traditions such as Buddhism and Hinduism, Protestant and Catholic differences look like a family squabble. Differences do exist, but efforts have brought appreciation of the richness held in common to clearer focus. One area of interest in Protestantism today is what Catholics call "spirituality." I would like to point out that an example of Catholic spirituality which Meland, a Protestant, helped explain and which might be a reciprocal possibility for Protestant "spirituality."

In the mystical tradition of the Roman Catholic Church after the Reformation, Ignatius of Loyola, a 16th century mystic, drew upon the tradition of the "discernment of spirits." In his "Rules for the Discernment of Spirits" in the *Spiritual Exercises of St. Ignatius*, St. Ignatius talks about the interior movements of the spirits in the exercitant. The discernment process is a self-monitored and experiential procedure under the direction of an objective director. Discernment is a technical procedure. The reason is that the movements of God within the person are ever so slight. Ignatius provides help for the director in what should be looked for. Ignatius draws upon images to help explain what occurs. At one point,[9] Ignatius says that the interior action of God through the good or evil spirit upon the soul can be likened to a drop of water falling upon an object. If the action is like water penetrating a sponge, the action is from the good spirit. "The action of the good angel is delicate, gentle, delightful." If the action is like water falling upon a rock, that is the evil spirit. "The action of the evil spirit is violent, noisy, and disturbing." The action of God is not jarring but ever so slight and gentle. The rough but almost imperceptible jarring of the soul to the efforts of the spirit is a sign of evil. What is presented is the interior working by God as one of gentleness.

One of the striking qualities of Meland's description about God's work in creativity and in revelation is that of gentleness. When ruptures of relationships occur which are violent, God comes in the gentleness of that experience. Meland's treatment of death is an outstanding presentation of that fact. Perhaps as outstanding and more to the nature of God himself, Meland's portrayal of the Suffering Servant as the revelation of God in Jesus is a statement about God's workings with us. The Suffering Servant shows God as suffering love. The gentle, sensitive, suffering quality of love in the face of violence sustains relationships and draws others in love. Love draws love in gentle freedom.

From the different perspectives, the convergence of God's working upon the individual as characteristically gentle is remarkably similar. Perhaps, and I believe this to be true, there are closer parallels operative in both Protestant and Catholic traditions that will bear closer examination. I might add that Ignatius' approach to the discernment of spirits seems very appreciative in the manner of Meland. Further examination of the Appreciative Awareness might enhance the personal, social, and cultural aspects of spirituality for Catholics, perhaps even giving fuller scope to the discernment of spirits conceived by Ignatius. The theological convergence swings both ways and can enhance both traditions from their already existing states of development.[10]

In one sense, continuous exploration and expansion of Meland's thought is possible. It is not important that Meland has not covered the entire field but that he has done well what he has begun. At times, it seemed that Meland almost sacrificed depth in his work in order to present the relational-contextual perspective which generated his own belief. Further work of specification is left for others. The legacy of Meland is after all the persuasive power of his thought and insights to articulate our experience and faith. Internal criteria of adequacy and coherence must be argued about and applied. Truth claims must be submitted to analysis. External criteria will be the power to persuade others to share the vision and its closeness to the truth that we experience almost independent of adequacy and coherence. But if the process of total conversion will be there, both criteria must be fulfilled. Meland exemplifies both. If theology is understood as: faith seeking understanding, at some point, a theologian must be able to be judged as one who provides the other half of the double-edged challenge of theology: faith finding understanding today. Meland has done it and deserves that attention.

NOTES

CONSIDERATIONS

[1] David Hall, *Process Studies*, vol. 7, no. 2 (1978), p. 112. This is a critical review of Meland's *Fallible Forms and Symbols*. It is one of the best reviews of Meland's work.

[2] John Cobb, Jr., and David Griffin, *Process Theology* (Philadelphia: Westminster, 1976), pp. 174–75, 178.

[3] Jane Dillenberger, *Secular Art with Sacred Themes* (New York: Abingdon Press, 1969), p. 12.

[4] William James, *The Varieties of Religious Experience* (New York: Macmillan, 1969).

[5] Erik Erikson, *Identity, Youth, and Crisis* (New York: Norton, 1968).

[6] Jean Piaget, *The Moral Development of the Child* (trans. Marjorie Gabain, New York: Free Press, 1965); John H. Flavell, *The Developmental Psychology of Jean Piaget* (New York: Van Nostrand, 1963).

[7] Lawrence Kohlberg has a number of articles, but a better guide is Ronald Duska and M. Whelan, *Moral Development* (New York: Paulist Press, 1975).

[8] See David Tracy, *Blessed Rage for Order* (New York: Seabury, 1975); also Lewis Ford, *The Lure of God* (Philadelphia: Fortress Press, 1978); and Raymond Brown, "Hermeneutics," *Jerome Biblical Commentary* (New Jersey: Prentice-Hall, 1968), 605-23; and Bernard Lonergan *Method in Theology* (New York: Herder & Herder, 1972).

[9] *Spiritual Exercises of St. Ignatius,* (trans. Louis J. Phul, Westminster: The Neman Press, 1963), No. 335.7.

[10] I have begun to develop this dimension. See my article J.J. Mueller, S.J., "Prayer and the Mental Prayer Tradition," in *Review for Religious*, to be published.

GLOSSARY OF MELAND'S TERMS

Appreciative Consciousness (or Appreciative Awareness): The Appreciative Consciousness is defined over against the Rational and Moral Consciousnesses. "Appreciative Awareness is the attitude of trust assuming an explicit cognitive concern." (FC, 120) The Appreciative Awareness is the conscious attention of the self, including the feelings and emotions, to the interrelationship of the self to the contextual environing event. "The appreciative capacity becomes a form of energy affecting not only the structure of personality that embraces it, but also the structure of relations that defines the whole context of living in which this individual participates as a person." (FC, 175) In his classical definition, a quote from Meland's *Higher Education and the Human Spirit* (Chicago: University of Chicago Press; 1953, p. 63) is needed: Appreciative Awareness "is a regulative principle in thought which, as an orientation of the mind, can make for a maximum degree of receptivity to the datum under consideration on the principle that what is given may be more than what is immediately perceived, or more than one can think."

Church: The organization of a community within a cultural community, bearing and nurturing the revelation of historic events. (cf. FC, 145)

Constructive Theology: "A focusing of the theological interest upon immediate demands and concerns of living as these evoke and convey the realities of faith." (FFS, xiv)

Constructive Theology, The Method of: "It takes the immediacies of experience seriously as bearing depths of reality expressive simultaneously of an historical stream and of an ontological present, to which response the interpretation must be given. To this extent, a theology of culture relates the historical legacy transmitted through the church and to the accumulative thrust of the mythos." (FFS, 121)

Creative Passage: "The basic characterization of existence as it applies to all life, to all people, to all cultures." It is the "objective side" or empirical side of reality. The subjective side is the "stream of experience." God is of "a piece" with the Creative Passage. It is sometimes referred to as Ultimacy in relationships. "It is assumed that our immediacies occur and participate in a dimension of ultimacy." (FFS, xiii)

Culture: (shorthand definition) "Culture" connotes the total complex of human growth that has occurred within any clearly defined orbit of human association, expressing its prevailing sentiment, style, and way of life." (FFS, 155)

Cultus: "The Cult, or Cultus, is generally defined as a particular system of worship, including its body of belief, its organization, as well as its ceremonial." (FFS, 156)

Depth: The expression of the dimension of reality that extends beyond one's ability to exhaust it, especially rationally. "The realities of any experience are to be accounted deeper than, or in some aspects resistant to, man's power of observation and description." (RF, 93)

Ego Centrism. "Perverse assertiveness of the centered existence disregarding or betraying its communal ground which initiates the complex of human responses and behaviors which may rightfully be termed *sin.*" (RF, 245) Deficiency of empathy results in *schizophrenia* which is Meland's word for a failure of socialization or the subjective life turned in upon itself. (FC, 136)

Elemental Dimension (Also called Creaturely Dimension): "Living with an awareness of the fact of birth and death, confronting man's existence, its range of opportunity for human fulfillment, not only within these acknowledged limits defined by birth and death, but with creaturely feelings appropriate to them." (FFS, 165)

Empirical Realism: "A process orientation of inquiry looking to the lived experience." (FFS, xiii)

Faith: An initial situation of depth which precedes and underlies the reasoning mind. It takes the form of immanent and transcendent.

Faith as Immanent: "The condition of trust which comes to dominate the psychical experience of a people, or a person, preparing them to confront the ultimate mystery of experience; or simply to find innumerable instances which awaken man to his limits, his creaturehood, his dependence." (RF, 215)

Faith as Transcendent. A gift of grace which "reclaims man from the alienations of self-experience." It is a conscious commitment to the creative ground which claims us. (RF, 217)

Faith, Witnesses of (also Orbits of Meaning, and Vortices of Experience): "By orbit of meaning I refer to the cycle of responses giving rise to a complex of symbols and signs, expressed or anticipated, which contribute to a sense of orientation and familiarity in one's mode of existence." The Culture, Cultus, and Individual are the three clearest witnesses, orbits, or vortices to the Christian legacy in the Western World. (FFS, 173).

Freedom: "Awareness of possibilities and a capacity to respond to them selectively." (FC, 175)

Gestalt of Grace: "The movement of spirit in relations that have been formed out of a common witness to the Christ. It is a holistic instance of New Being wherein the structure of spirit has become luminous in historic events. . . a transparent structure which allows the New Being to 'shine through.'" (RF, 300-1)

Goodness Not Our Own: Meland's empirical, experiential description of the reality of God in the Creative Passage.

Imago Dei. The theological expression of the relationship of the human person to God. The relationships given at birth are connected to this expression and are threefold in their demand upon every individual: I am made for God, for others, for my self. (RF, 207)

Mythos: The accumulative psychical energy of faith in the past that exists through myth. It is "a non-cognitive mode of meaning and motivation in the living structure of experience of any people or culture." Its rational counterpart is Logos. (FFS, 103)

New Creation: The new creation of life in the Christ-event whereby the person is grasped by "a goodness not our own"; and the vital energy released becomes a new resource of grace and judgment. (RF, 217)

New Realism: Meland's phrase for the Age of Power that follows Newtonian mechanics. It takes experience seriously and the novel event such that ultimacies and immediacies traffic together.

Process: This word stands both for a philosophy and the developing structured event. As a Philosophy, Meland understands it to be Bergson, James, Dewey and Whitehead who reappropriates their insights. It is therefore a wide swath of thinkers. As a developing structured event, Meland is not satisfied with "process" as expressive of "becoming": "It includes other themes than process which are more important, such as 'dimensional meaning,' 'contextual relations,' and 'emerging events.' (FFS, xii)

spirit: (small 's'): The dimension of depth in the person referred to as the "realm of the spirit" which issues in freedom. "A quality of being which arises out of a particular depth of sensitivity in relations." (RF, 234)

Spirit: (capital "S"): The Holy Spirit also called the "discerned nature" of God working in the ambiguity of human limitations. (FC, 216)

Structure of Experience: "A static characterization of the persisting valuations of the culture which carry the net result of the cultural history into the present." (FC, 102)

Symbolization: "The procedure of creating meaning and of interrelating meanings through communicable symbols." It is the process by which the individual internalizes the meanings and resources of the culture. (FC, 140)

Ultimate Efficacy: "It connotes a continuous thrust of the Creative Passage, and is thus simultaneously the present, inclusive of the legacy of the past inherent in its structure of experience, together with what is prescient of its future range. . . Ultimacy can be conceived of under the aegis of 'importance'; i.e. as a dimension of the relational ground of every existent event. . . offering potential fulfillment of its intention. . . or what persists as a concrete destiny." (FFS, xiii)

SELECTED BIBLIOGRAPHY OF WORKS BY BERNARD E. MELAND

In Chronological Order: 1929—52

Modern Man's Worship: A Search for Reality in Religion. New York and London: Harper and Brothers, 1934.

American Philosophies of Religion (with Henry Nelson Wieman). Chicago and New York: Willet, Clark and Company, 1936; New York: Harper, 1948.

"The Faith of a Mystical Naturalist," Review of Religion, I (1937), 270—78.

The Church and Adult Education. New York: American Association for Adult Education, 1939.

Seeds of Redemption. New York: Macmillan, 1947.

America's Spiritual Culture. New York: Harper & Brothers, 1948.

The Reawakening of Christian Faith. New York: Macmillan, 1949.

1953—64.

Faith and Culture. New York: Oxford University Press, 1953.

Higher Education and the Human Spirit. Chicago: University of Chicago Press, 1963; paperback, Chicago: Seminary Cooperative Bookstore, 1965.

"Interpreting the Christian Faith within a Philosophical Framework," *Journal of Religion,* 33 (1953), 87-102.

"Analogy and Myth in Post-Liberal Theology," *Perkins School of Theology Journal* 15 (1962), 19—27.

The Realities of Faith: The Revolution in Cultural Forms. New York: Oxford University Press, 1962; paperback, Chicago: Seminary Cooperative Bookstore, 1970.

"The Root and Form of Wieman's Thought," *The Empirical Theology of Henry Nelson Wieman,* ed. Robert W. Bretall. New York: Macmillan, 1963, 44—68.

"A Post-Retreat Comment to Professor Haroutunian," *Criterion* 3 (1964), 11 f.

"How Is Culture a Source for Theology?" *Criterion* 3 (1964), 10—21.

"New Perspectives on Nature and Grace," *The Scope of Grace*, ed. Philip Hefner, Philadelphia: Fortress Press, 1964, 143—61.

1964—76.

The Secularizaton of Modern Cultures. New York: Oxford University Press, 1966.

"Mytho-Poetic Dimension of Faith Within Modern Culture," *Criterion* 6 (1967), 5—7.

"Credo," *Criterion* 7 (1968), 29—32.

"The Structure of Christian Faith," *Religion in Life* 37 (1968), 551—62.

"Can Empirical Theology Learn Something from Phenomenology?" *The Future of Empirical Theology*, ed. B. Meland. Chicago: University of Chicago Press, 1969.

The Future of Empirical Theology (ed.) Chicago: University of Chicago Press, 1969.

"Analogy and Myth in Postliberal Theology," *Process Philosophy and Christian Thought*, ed. Delwin Brown, Ralph E. James, Jr. and Gene Reeves. Indianapolis: Bobbs-Merrill Company, Inc., 1971, 116—27.

"Evolution and the Imagery of Religious Thought: From Darwin to Whitehead," *Process Philosophy and Christian Thought*, ed. Delwin Brown, Ralph E. James, Jr., and Gene Reeves. Indianapolis: Bobbs-Merrill Co., Inc., 1971, 411-30.

"Faith and Formative Imagery of Our Time," *Process Theology*, ed. Ewert H. Cousins. New York: Newman Press, 1971, 37—45.

"The New Creation," *Process Theology*, ed. Ewert H. Cousins. New York: Newman Press, 1971, 191—202.

"The Unifying Moment" (review of Craig R. Eisendrath's *The Unifying Moment: The Psychological Philosophy of William James and Alfred North Whitehead), Process Studies* 3 (1973), 285—90.

"Grace, A Dimension of Nature?" *The Journal of Religion 54* (1974), 119—37.

Fallible Forms and Symbols: Discourses on Method for a Theology of Culture: Philadelphia: Fortress Press, 1976.

There is a complete bibliography of both primary and secondary sources on Bernard E. Meland in *Process Studies,* 1975, 285—302. It combines a previous bibliograpy of 1964 in *Quest* with the recent material and has the added benefit of Meland's inclusion of other unpublished works.

SELECTED GENERAL BIBLIOGRAPHY

Ahlstrom, Sydney E. *A Religious History of the American People.* New Haven: Yale, 1972.

_____. *Theology in America.* New York: Bobbs-Merrill, 1967.

Barbour, Ian. *Myths, Models, and Paradigms.* New York: Harper, 1974.

Berger, Peter. *The Sacred Canopy.* New York: Doubleday, 1969.

Bergson, Henri. *Creative Evolution.* Trans. Arthur Mitchell. New York: Random House, 1944.

Bretall, Robert (ed). *The Empirical Theology of Henry Nelson Wieman.* New York: Macmillan, 1963.

Brown, Delwin, Ralph E. James, Jr., and Gene Reeves (eds). *Process Philosophy and Christian Thought.* Indianapolis: Bobbs-Merrill, 1971.

Brown, Raymond, "Hermeneutics," *Jerome Biblical Commentary.* New Jersey: Prentice-Hall, 1968, 605-23.

Cobb, John B. *The Structure of Christian Existence.* Philadelphia: Westminster, 1967.

_____ *A Christian Natural Theology.* Philadelphia: Westminster, 1965.

_____. *Christ in a Pluralistic Age.* Philadelphia: Westminster, 1975.

Cobb, John B., and David Griffin. *Process Theology*. Philadelphia: Westminster, 1976.

Cousins, Ewert (ed). *Process Theology*. New York: Newman, 1971.

Dewey, John. *Experience and Nature*. LaSalle, Illinois: Open Court, 1971.

Dillenberger, Jane. *Secular Art with Sacred Themes*. New York: Abingdon, 1969.

Dunne, John. *A Search for God in Time and Memory*. New York: Macmillan, 1965.

Duska, Ronald and M. Whelan. *Moral Development*. New York: Paulist, 1975.

Eisendrath, Craig R. *The Unifying Moment*. Cambridge: Harvard University Press, 1971.

Ellis, John Tracy. *American Catholicism*. Chicago: University of Chicago, 1969.

Emmett, Dorothy. *The Nature of Metaphysical Thinking*. London: Macmillan, 1949.

Erikson, Erik. *Identity, Youth, and Crisis*. New York: Norton, 1968.

Ford, Lewis. *The Lure of God*. Philadelphia: Fortress Press, 1978.

Gelpi, Donald. *Charism and Sacrament*. New York: Paulist Press, 1976.

—————. *Experiencing God*. New York: Paulist Press, 1978.

Gilkey, Langdon. *Catholicism Confronts Modernity*. New York: Seabury Press, 1975.

—————. *Naming the Whirlwind*. New York: Bobbs-Merrill, 1969.

Gragg, Alan. *Charles Hartshorne*. Waco: Word, 1973.

Hart, Ray. *Unfinished Man and the Imagination*. New York: Herder & Herder, 1968.

Hartshorne, Charles. *The Divine Relativity*. New Haven: Yale, 1948.

—————. *A Natural Theology for Our Time.* LaSalle: Open Court, 1967.

—————. *Reality as Social Process.* Boston: Beacon, 1953.

Harvey, Van A. *The Historian and the Believer.* New York: Macmillan, 1966.

Hefner, Philip, "Theological Worldliness: Bernard Meland's Contribution to Theological Methodology," *Quest* 8 (1964), 26—32.

Heidegger, Martin. *Introduction to Metaphysics.* New Haven: Yale, 1959.

James, William. *Pluralistic Universe.* New York: Longmans, Green, 1909.

—————. *The Principles of Psychology.* 2 Vols. New York: Henry Holt & Co., 1890.

—————. *The Varieties of Religious Experience.* New York: Collier, 1961.

—————. *The Will to Believe and Other Essays in Popular Philosophy.* New York: Dover, 1956.

Kasper, Walter. *Jesus the Christ.* New York: Paulist, 1976.

Kuhn, Thomas. *The Structure of Scientific Revolution.* Chicago: University of Chicago Press, 1962.

Langer, Susanne. *Philosophy in a New Key.* New York: Penguin, 1948.

Lonergan, Bernard. *Insight: A Study of Human Understanding.* London: Longmans, Green & Co., 1957.

—————. *Method in Theology.* New York: Herder and Herder, 1972.

Loomer, Bernard. *"Two Conceptions of Power,"* Process Studies, Vol. 6 (Spring, 1976), 5—32.

Lynch, William. *Christ and Apollo.* New York: Mentor, 1960.

Maslow, Abraham. *Toward a Psychology of Being.* New York: Van Nostrand, 1962.

McAvoy, Thomas T. *A History of the Catholic Church in the U.S.* Notre Dame: University of Notre Dame Press, 1969.

Miller, R.C. *The American Spirit in Theology.* United Church Press, 1974.

Neumann, Erich. *The Origins and History of Consciousness.* Trans. R.F.C. Hull. Princeton: Billingen, 1954.

Ogden, Schubert. *Christ Without Myth.* New York: Harper, 1961.

——————— *The Reality of God and Other Essays.* New York: Harper, 1964.

Otto, Rudolf. *The Idea of the Holy.* Trans. John W. Harvey. New York: Oxford, 1950.

Peirce, Charles S. *Selected Writings. New York: Dover, 1966.*

Peden, W. Creighton, "Meland's Philosophical Method" Part One, *The Iliff Review,* 31 (Spring, 1974), 43—53; Part Two (Fall, 1974), 35—45.

Piaget, Jean. *The Moral Development of the Child.* Trans. Marjorie Gabain. New York: Free Press, 1965.

Price, Lucien. *Dialogues of Alfred North Whitehead.* New York: Mentor, 1956.

Puhl, Louis J. (trans.) *The Spiritual Exercises of St. Ignatius.* Westminster: Newman Press, 1963.

Rahner, Karl. *Hearers of the Word.* Trans. Michael Richards. New York: Herder & Herder, 1969.

——————— *Theological Investigations.* Vol. 4. Baltimore: Helicon, 1966.

Ricoeur, Paul. *The Symbolism of Evil.* Trans. E. Buchanan. Boston: Beacon, 1967.

Royce, Josiah. *The Problem of Christianity.* 2 vols. Chicago: Regnery, 1968.

Schillebeeckx, Edward. *Christ: The Experience of Jesus as Lord.* New York: Seabury, 1980.

Schilpp, Paul A. *The Philosophy of Alfred North Whitehead.* New York: Tudor, 1951.

Schoof, T.M. *A Survey of Catholic Theology 1800—1970.* New York: Paulist, 1970.

Sherburne, Donald. *A Key to Whitehead's Process and Reality*. New York: Macmillan, 1966.

Smith, John E. *The Analogy of Experience*. New York: Harper, 1973.

——————. *Experience and God*. New York: Oxford, 1968.

Sobrino, Jon. *Christology at the Crossroads*. New York: Orbis, 1978.

Sontag, Frederick and J.K. Roth. *The American Religious Experience. New York: Harper, 1972.*

Spiegler, Gerhard, "Ground-Task-End of Theology in the Thought of Bernard E. Meland," *Criterion* 3 (1964), 34—38.

Tillich, Paul. *Systematic Theology*. Chicago: University of Chicago, 1967.

——————— *Theology of Culture*. New York: Oxford University Press, 1964.

Toulmin, Stephen. *The Uses of Argument*. New York: Cambridge University Press, 1958.

Tracy, David. *Blessed Rage for Order*. New York: Seabury, 1975.

Whitehead, Alfred North. *Adventures of Ideas*. New York: Mentor, 1933.

——————. *Process and Reality*. New York: Free Press, 1929.

——————. *Religion in the Making*. New York: Macmillan, 1926.

——————. *Symbolism*. New York: Capricorn, 1927.

Wieman, Henry Nelson. *The Source of Human Good*. Carbondale, Illinois: Southern Illinois University Press, 1946.

Wilder, Amos. *Theopoetics: Theology and the Imagination*. Philadelphia: Fortress Press, 1976.

Williams, Daniel Day. *The Spirit and Forms of Love*. New York: Harper, 1968.

——————— "The Theology of Bernard E. Meland," *Criterion* 3 (1964), 3—9.

Williamson, C.M. Abstract of Peden, "Meland's Philosophical Method—Part One," *Process Studies* 5 (Summer, 1975), 151.

_____ Abstract of Peden, "Meland's Philosophical Method—Part Two," *Process Studies* 5 (Summer, 1975), 152.

_____. "The Road to Realism," *Criterion* 3 (1964), 22—24.

Yonan, E.A., "The Theology of Bernard Meland," *Quest* 8 (1964), 13—25.